Diagonal (or On-Point) Set

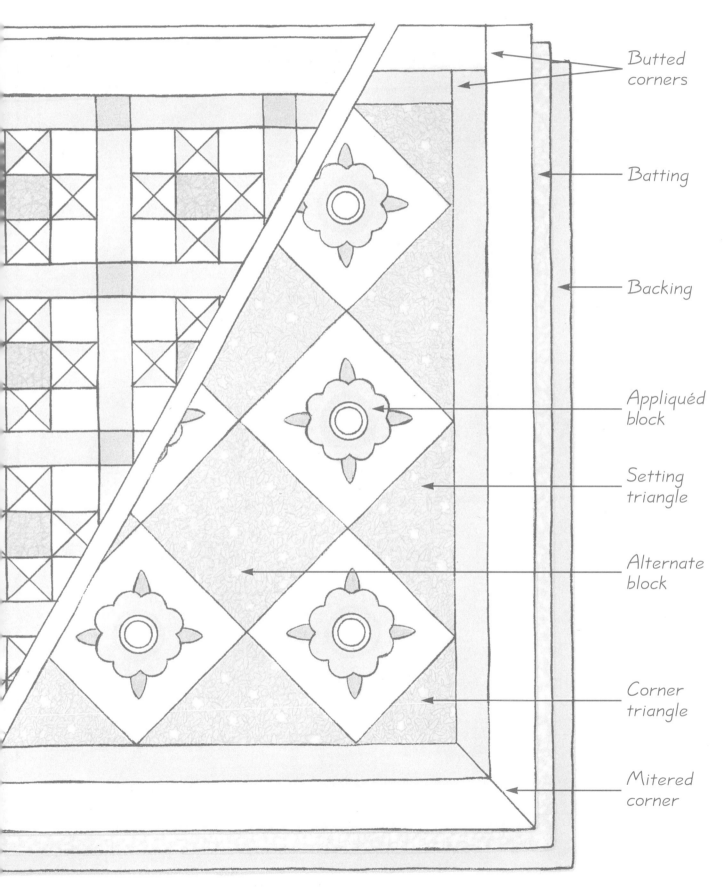

Butted corners

Batting

Backing

Appliquéd block

Setting triangle

Alternate block

Corner triangle

Mitered corner

Rodale's Successful Quilting Library™

Perfect Piecing

Karen Costello Soltys,
Editor

Rodale Press, Inc.
Emmaus, Pennsylvania

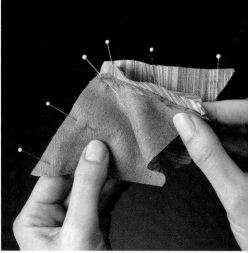

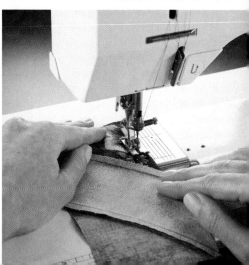

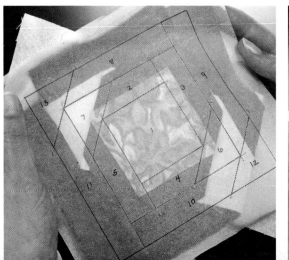

OUR PURPOSE

*"We inspire and enable people to improve
their lives and the world around them."*

The writers and editors who compiled this book have tried to make all of the contents as accurate and as correct as possible. Text and illustrations have all been carefully checked and cross-checked. However, due to the variability of materials, personal skill, and so on, Rodale Press does not assume any responsibility for any injuries suffered or for damages or other losses incurred that result from the material presented herein. All instructions and illustrations should be carefully studied and clearly understood before beginning any project.

Printed in the United States of America on acid-free ∞, recycled ♲ paper

Editor: Karen Costello Soltys
Designer: Sue Gettlan
Book Layout/Illustrator:
    Christopher Rhoads
Illustrator: Mario Ferro
Photographer: Mitch Mandel
Stylist: Stan Green
Hand Model: Anne Cassar
Copy Editor: Erana Bumbardatore
Manufacturing Coordinator:
    Patrick Smith
Indexer: Nanette Bendyna
Editorial assistance: Susan Nickol
    and Jodi Rehl
Editor photograph: John Hamel
Endsheet Illustrator: Doug Knutson

On the cover: Scrapaholic's Delight
by Gloria J. Evans of Naperville, Illinois

Rodale Home and Garden Books
Vice President and Editorial Director:
    Margaret J. Lydic
Managing Editor: Suzanne Nelson
Art Director: Paula Jaworski
Associate Art Director: Mary Ellen Fanelli
Studio Manager: Leslie Keefe
Copy Director: Dolores Plikaitis
Book Manufacturing Director:
    Helen Clogston

We're happy to hear from you.

For questions or comments concerning the editorial content of this book, please write to:

Rodale Press, Inc.
Book Readers' Service
33 East Minor Street
Emmaus, PA 18098

For more information about Rodale Press and the books and magazines we publish, visit our World Wide Web site at:
http://www.rodalepress.com

Library of Congress Cataloging-in-Publication Data

Rodale's successful quilting library.
    p. cm.
Includes index.
ISBN 0-87596-760-4 (hc: v. 1:alk paper)
1. Quilting. 2. Patchwork. I. Soltys,
Karen Costello. II. Rodale Press.
TT835.R622 1997
746.46'041—dc21   96-51316

Distributed in the book trade
by St. Martin's Press

4 6 8 10 9 7 5 3   hardcover

Contents

Introduction

I made my first quilt, a twin-size sampler, in 1979. Since that time, I've learned a lot about quiltmaking in classes and from fellow quiltmakers. One of the most enjoyable aspects of quilt-making for me is the camaraderie and selfless sharing that goes on among quilters. We share ideas, fabrics, tips, and more.

While I was fortunate to be exposed to some really terrific quilting teachers—and friends—over the years, I've also seen my share of patterns, articles, and books that didn't always provide me with the detailed information I wanted about a quilt project. Sometimes the directions weren't clear. Other times, I simply wished for more in-depth explanations. I wanted to know how to do things the right way and not be left guessing.

That's why it was so exciting for me to work on this book. You see, I don't profess to be the expert who knows all the answers for making perfect patchwork. But I know a lot of wonderful, award-winning quiltmakers, sought-after teachers, and all-star authors who do! And what's great is that they agreed to share their best tips, techniques, and secrets for perfect piecing with you.

Our expert team of creative consultants—Debra Wagner, Sharyn Craig, and Dixie Haywood—are all well known, not only for their glorious quilts but also for their enthusiasm in sharing quiltmaking ideas with their students. And they had no shortage of ideas for this book, as you'll see when you glance through the table of contents. Their input helped us shape the content of this book, and their contributions were invaluable.

The team of experts who wrote the book—Jane Hall, Dixie Haywood, and Janet Wickell—took our outlines and ideas and set out to present everything from choosing the right tools to making accurate paper foundations in clear, easy-to-understand, step-by-step lessons. Of course they each added their own dose of tips and secrets to success along the way. In fact, they were so full of good ideas that in some cases, we just didn't have enough room to share them all!

What's more, each technique in this book has been editor tested. All the samples you see in the nearly 300 step-by-step photographs were made here at Rodale Press by me and several other quilters on our staff. We figured there was no better way to make sure that the directions were

clearly explained than by trying each technique ourselves.

Whether your idea of perfect piecing is completing a crib quilt that will be cuddled for years by a grandchild or piecing a masterpiece worthy of your guild's top prize for patchwork, I hope you'll enjoy using this book. No matter how long you've been quilting or what your skill level is, I'm confident you'll find new and

helpful information, plus lots of photos that take the mystery out of supposedly tricky techniques. My hope is that you'll find dozens of tips that will make you stop and say, "Wow—I didn't know that!" I know I did.

Karen Soltys

Karen Costello Soltys
Editor

1 Quilters often spend a great deal of money to acquire sewing machines with every option imaginable, but forget about one tiny, inexpensive item that's essential for good stitches—the needles. Sewing machine needles stitch best when sharp, so get in the habit of replacing the needle often. Dull or burred needles often announce their presence by becoming noisy. Replace them at once.

2 Press seam allowances toward the darker fabric unless there is a good reason to do otherwise. For instance, in the illustration below, the seam allowances of the side patches are pressed toward the lighter fabric so there will be less bulk underneath the narrow center piece.

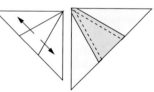

Press to avoid bulk

3 A 3- or 4-inch piece of masking tape makes a great catchall for threads and bits of scrap fabric. Just make a loop of tape with the sticky side of the tape facing outward and stick it wherever you like to catch snippets of thread, scraps, and even stray pins or needles. When you are finished working for the day, just pull off any pins you want to keep and toss the tape away.

4 For quick and easy measuring, place a self-stick ruler at the front edge of the mat or table underneath your sewing machine. If you can't find a self-stick ruler, you can make one by using a regular ruler and two-sided tape.

5 In addition to keeping your scissors sharp, check to be sure they cut straight. Scissors that are dull or have been dropped may not cut a true line. Check by cutting along a stripe or a plaid to see if the scissors follow the line in a smooth cut from base to point. If they don't, a professional scissors sharpener may be able to align the blades.

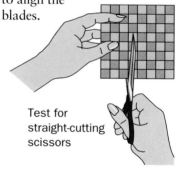

Test for straight-cutting scissors

6 Whenever you start a new piecing project, find a box large enough to hold and organize all of the cut pieces for the quilt, plus any templates, and the pattern or book you're using. Being organized means more time can be spent sewing—not searching!

7 When you mark a line for a ¼-inch seam allowance on your sewing machine, be sure to include the actual width of your stitching line. If your seam allowance does not include the width of your stitches, you'll be altering the size of the finished patchwork at every seam. For example, if there are five seams across a block, you can sometimes remove as much as ⁵⁄₃₂ inch from one block.

8 Avoid pressing a bias edge with hot steam until you have stitched it to another patch. Instead, finger press it by placing the sewn seam on a firm surface with the darker patch on top. Peel back the dark patch and run your thumbnail along the ditch of the seam.

Bias edges

Finger press

9 Piece a practice block first in order to determine which piecing order you prefer and which direction you want the seams to face. Once you know how you want your block to go together, machine piece blocks in units so that each type of unit is completed before you go on to the next. Then assemble the various units into completed blocks.

10 If your sewing machine has a half-speed setting, use it to sew accurate seams at a slower, more methodical pace. This feature is especially helpful for curved seams where you need to go slowly, remove pins, and pivot often.

11 If your finished block isn't quite square, try

correcting the problem with pressing. Cut a square of gridded or plain freezer paper to the exact *unfinished* size your block should be, and press the waxy side down on your ironing board. Place your block on top of the paper, and align the corners with those of the paper. Pin the block to the ironing board to keep it from moving. Align the edges of block and paper, and pin through those areas, too. Use steam, or spray the block lightly with sizing and press to help it retain its square shape.

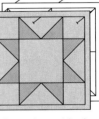

Squaring a block

12 One of the great debates among quilters is whether or not it's okay to sew over pins. If it's necessary to stitch over pins, do so *slowly* and use thin pins to reduce your chances of hitting one with the needle. Discard bent pins immediately—they can interfere with the stitch and break a needle, which may throw off the timing of your machine.

13 Ask your sewing machine dealer about buying machine needles in bulk. Bulk needles are less expensive per needle than those sold in small packages, and you won't find yourself stranded without a needle when the stores are closed.

14 A straight-stitch throat plate makes machine stitching more precise because it eliminates the play around the needle as it enters the fabric. The larger hole on the standard zigzag throat plate allows the fabric to flex as the needle pierces it, which some-

times causes gathering at the start of stitching. Straight-stitch plates are available for most types of machines. (Remember to remove them when moving the needle position or zig-zagging!)

15 Grid-method triangle squares and quarter-square triangles can be a great time-saver. Make them accurate, too, by drawing the grid on paper. It's easier and more accurate than drawing on fabric. Place two pieces of fabric right sides together, pin the drawing on top, and stitch ¼ inch on each side of every diagonal line, as usual. Cut apart on all lines and remove the papers. This is so accurate you won't have to waste time truing up squares as is often the case when the grid is drawn directly on the fabric.

Grid method

16 Whenever four or more seams come together at one point, press the seams open, borrowing a tailor's trick. Dip one finger into a bowl of water and apply just a dab of moisture right into the area where multiple seam allowances come together and fan out. The few drops of water will help compress the seams and make them lie flatter when you press them.

Fan center join

17 Try this for complex machine piecing with many points or long, thin shapes: Mark the seam

intersections with dots and sew from dot to dot. Or, draw on complete seam lines and stitch on the drawn lines for accurate piecing. Another option is to use freezer paper templates as foundations for these shapes. Cut them *without* seam allowances and sew right at the edge of the paper for precise piecing.

Freezer paper templates

18 When piecing strips of fabric together by machine, try this pressing technique to make sure the seams lie flat and the strips will be straight. Lay the two fabric strips on your ironing board with the seam lying away from you and the darker fabric on top. Press the seam to set the stitches. Open the strips and press the seam again, placing the iron on the lighter fabric and pressing—without steam—toward the darker fabric. This two-step process will make your strips straight, without the "rainbow" effect that can come from rippling, pleating, or puckering seams.

19 When doing repetitive jobs like rotary cutting or sewing, stop every 20 minutes for a mini-break. Stretch your arms, shrug your shoulders, and rest your eyes by changing their focus across the room or looking out a window.

20 Use the best sewing machine, scissors, pins, thread, rulers, and rotary cutters you can afford. It is not necessary to have "top of the line" tools and equipment to piece well, but it is important to have reliable, accurate tools to produce precise, smooth pieces. You and your quilts are worth it!

Tools of *the Trade*

I t's a simple idea, but it's true—you get the best results when you use the right tools for the task. And taking this age-old wisdom one step further, you'll get the best from your tools when you take time to organize them so they're always within easy reach.

Getting Ready

Organize your work area and supplies for easy access. When piecing, you'll need to move back and forth from the sewing machine to the iron frequently, so try to set your space up so you can reach both from the same seat. One easy solution is to use a swivel office chair for sewing, with an ironing board lowered to sitting height right next to your sewing table.

By keeping your threads, bobbins, pins, and other necessities organized and handy, you'll be able to spend your time piecing your quilt, not hunting for misplaced notions. Quilting supplies (especially fabrics!) have a way of quickly filling your sewing space. Plan ahead to avoid unnecessary clutter. See-through plastic boxes make good, stackable storage containers and help you group small, related items. Remember—nobody has a bumper sticker that says the quilter with the most clutter wins!

What You'll Need

Sewing machine

Size 80/12 universal or size 11 machine quilting needles

Silk pins and pincushion

Rotary cutter, mat, and rulers

Fabric and craft scissors

Seam ripper

100% cotton sewing thread

Template materials

Size 10 sharp needles (for hand piecing)

Thimble (for hand piecing)

Iron and ironing board

¼" presser foot (optional)

Selecting Your Basic Tools

Sewing Machines

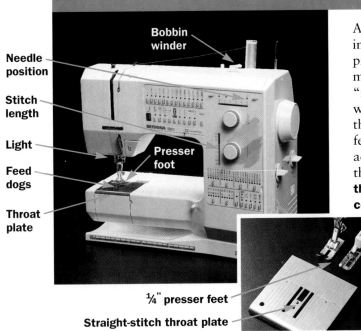

Needle position

Stitch length

Light

Feed dogs

Throat plate

Bobbin winder

Presser foot

¼" presser feet

Straight-stitch throat plate

Any straight-stitch sewing machine in good working order is suitable for piecing. If you're purchasing a new machine, consider one with a "needle-down" feature. Machines with this feature always stop with the needle in the fabric—a handy feature that prevents pieces from inadvertently slipping out from under the presser foot. **A straight-stitch throat plate is helpful, too, as it encourages consistent feeding and prevents fabric from being snarled in the feed dogs.**

A ¼-inch foot helps ensure an accurate seam allowance. If one isn't available for your machine, purchase a generic version, such as Little Foot.

Tip

Canned air blows the lint away from hard-to-reach parts of your sewing machine.

Pins & Pincushions

Tip

A magnetic wand is another handy tool. Sweep it across your sewing area to pick up stray pins after sewing.

Super-thin silk pins are best for pinning patchwork, since they glide into fabric easily and stay put until you remove them. Some quilters prefer pins with **glass ball or flower heads** because they're easy to handle and their visibility makes them less likely to be left behind in the work.

Wool pincushions aren't just decorative. They contain natural lanolin, which is gentle on pins. Another popular option is a **magnetic pin holder.** The magnetic base prevents pins from straying, but it causes more wear and tear on pins because pins scrape against one another.

Rotary-Cutting Supplies

Tip

Purchase the largest mat that is practical for your sewing area. Store it flat and away from sunlight and high temperatures.

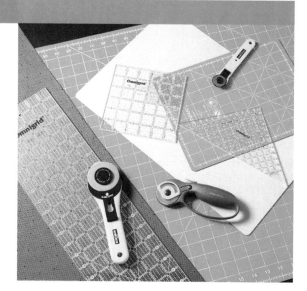

A rotary cutter is a must for quick-piecing techniques. **Cutters come in different sizes and with different handle types.** Choose one that feels comfortable to hold. All are razor sharp, so use them carefully. And be sure to use **a self-healing cutting mat** to protect your furniture and the rotary blade.

You'll also need an **acrylic ruler specifically designed for rotary cutting.** A 6 × 24-inch ruler marked in ⅛-inch increments and with 30, 45, and 60 degree markings is a worthwhile investment.

Scissors & Snips

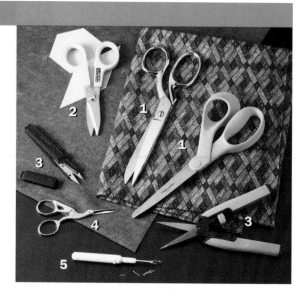

Reserve a pair of good quality 7- or 8-inch **dressmaker's shears (1)** for cutting fabric. **Craft scissors (2)** come in handy for cutting both paper patterns and cardboard or plastic templates. A pair of **thread snips (3)** or **embroidery scissors (4)** is a must to keep by your sewing machine for trimming threads—a task that will dull your fabric shears.

And, as much as we hate to admit it, everyone needs at least one **seam ripper (5).** Look for one with an extra-fine head that will slip easily under stitches.

Thread

Choose a thread that is compatible with the fiber content of your fabrics. For most quilters, that means **100 percent cotton or cotton-covered polyester sewing thread.** Because they are more rigid, threads made with synthetic fibers may, over time, cut into cotton fabric where patches are joined.

For projects with a definite color scheme, you may want to use thread that closely matches the quilt's predominant shade—such as black for an Amish quilt. In general, neutral gray is a good option, since it blends well with most fabrics.

Thread that is cross-wound on the spool flows much more easily through the machine, relieving tension problems.

Hand-Piecing Tools

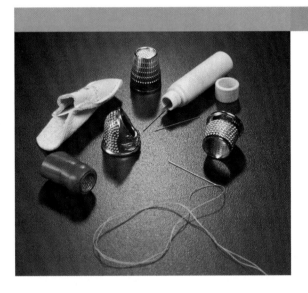

In addition to template materials and marking pencils, described in "Cutting Patches with Templates" on page 18, you'll also need a thimble and needles. (See page 117 for more information on needles.)

Try different types of thimbles until you find one that fits comfortably on the middle finger of your sewing hand. Leather thimbles are comfortable because they conform to your finger, but metal thimbles offer greater protection.

Iron

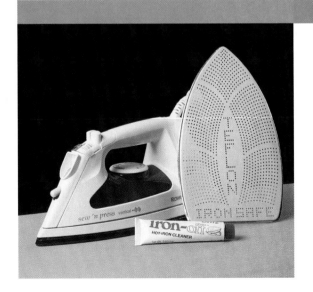

A good quality iron provides professional looking results. Keep your iron sole plate clean (especially if you use fusible web or interfacings) with **Iron Off,** or use a **protective sole plate covering.**

If you're in the market for a new iron, look for one that is easy to handle, has a cotton setting, but doesn't shut off automatically. Your ironing board should be firm, not overly padded. Choose a plain cotton cover rather than a Teflon one to absorb steam and let your fabric and blocks dry more easily.

TOOLS OF THE TRADE

Preparing Fabric
for Patchwork

P rewash or not? Ask any two quilters and you'll get two (maybe even three!) different answers. Here are some of the best reasons to test and prewash fabric before piecing: You can preshrink, check colorfastness, and remove any chemical coatings. Preparing fabric may take a bit of time, but it's not difficult, and it will help you avoid any unwelcome surprises that could occur after your project is finished.

Getting Ready

Some fabrics contain reactive dyes that chemically become a part of the fibers. These dyes (especially reds, blues, and purples) can bleed and stain other fabrics. Other colorants include dyes that are sealed on the surface of the fabric. These dyes can become suspended in wash water, but they generally don't stain other fabrics. Either dye type can cause *crocking*—the rubbing off of dyes from the fabric's surface during normal handling of dry fabric.

If you prewash, you won't have to worry about crocking. However, if you're tempted to skip prewashing because you don't plan to wash your project, test for crocking before making your final decision.

Rub a white cloth across a fabric you suspect may cause problems. Nearly all fabrics will show some amount of crocking, but if it's excessive, the dyes are more likely to transfer to other fabrics during handling. Avoid problems and prewash now.

What You'll Need

Unwashed 100% cotton fabrics

Mild soap or detergent

Glass bowl or large glass measuring cup

White terry cloth

Rust-proof safety pins

Fabric scissors

Iron and ironing board

Spray starch or sizing (optional)

Retayne (optional)

Synthrapol (optional)

Step-by-Step Fabric Preparation

1

Before tossing all quilt fabrics together in the washing machine, test a swatch of each for colorfastness. Snip off a ½-inch triangle from the selvage-edge corner of each fabric. **Pin a triangle from each fabric to its own swatch of white terry cloth. Drop a swatch into a clear glass container filled with warm, sudsy water and stir with a chopstick or drink stirrer.** If you have more than one glass container, you can test several fabrics at once. But don't put more than one cotton fabric in a container at a time.

Tip

If you have only one fabric to prewash, pin a terry cloth swatch to it and toss it in the washer. After washing, examine the terry cloth for dye transfer.

Let the container sit for about 5 minutes after stirring. Rinse the fabrics in warm water. **Unpin and check to see if dye has transferred onto the terry cloth.** If not, it's safe to wash the fabric with other colorfast pieces. Don't worry if the soapy water is tinged with dye. As long as the color didn't bleed onto the white terry cloth, the excess dye will simply wash away in the rinse water. If dye bleeds onto the terry cloth, however, repeat the test using the same ½-inch triangle pinned to a new terry cloth swatch.

3

If fabric still bleeds in a second color test, you have two choices: Don't use it in your quilt, or soak it in Retayne. Retayne, which is available at most quilt shops, is a dye fixative that helps set the dye and prevent it from bleeding or fading. Retayne is used in very hot water and takes about 20 minutes to activate. After soaking, rinse and toss fabric in the dryer. Follow the package directions for best results.

Tip

For precut squares, don't snip off triangles. Simply test and prewash each piece individually in the sink. Press dry.

4

Wash colorfast fabrics with a mild soap such as Orvus quilt soap (available at quilt shops), or another phosphate-free soap or detergent. Warm water is best for both washing and rinsing. If you don't have a warm wash cycle, use cold; never use hot water. To avoid wrinkles, stretching, and fraying, unfold and shake out fabrics before tossing them in the washer.

If the dye didn't bleed onto the terry cloth but tinged the soapy water, add Synthrapol to the wash cycle. It helps remove coatings and chemicals, plus it keeps dye particles suspended in the water so they won't stain other fabrics. Synthrapol is available from fabric dying supply companies.

Tip

To wash fat quarters and fat eighths, put pieces into a mesh lingerie bag to avoid excessive fraying and wrinkling.

5

Shake out each piece of fabric before placing it in the dryer—if they go in as a twisted clump, they'll likely come out that way. Remove threads that have unraveled and tangled during the wash. Set your dryer on its lowest heat cycle, and remove fabrics before they are completely dry to avoid annoying baked-in wrinkles and creases.

Tip

Set both your washer and dryer on the gentlest cycles to prevent fabric from fraying, tangling, and wrinkling.

6

Smooth out and stack small pieces as you remove them from the dryer. Press them right away so you're sure they're dry before storing to prevent mildew. **For long, damp yardages, drape them over the shower curtain rod or use skirt hangers to hang fabrics on a washline, door, or hook in your laundry room**—anything to keep pieces straight and wrinkle-free until you're ready to press the slightly damp fabric.

7

Set your iron on medium heat. **To avoid stretching the fabric grain, don't iron too vigorously.** If small pieces of fabric stretched in the wash, straighten them by gently pulling from opposite corners; press them into the correct shape. You can regain the stiffness and control new fabrics provide for cutting with spray starch or sizing.

Fold fabrics selvage to selvage, aligning edges so fabrics fold flat with no gaps or puckers along the folded edge. Make additional folds to fit your storage space.

Tip

Starched folds are hard to press away after being stored, so don't add starch (or sizing) until ready to use your fabric.

PREPARING FABRIC FOR PATCHWORK

Cutting Patches *with Templates*

Rotary cutters, with their quick and easy accuracy, have revolutionized quiltmaking. But templates should not be forgotten and abandoned, for they still have a place in a savvy quilter's bag of tricks. Templates can improve accuracy on intricate blocks, and they give you the opportunity to add creative touches that would be difficult to achieve with quick-cutting and -piecing techniques. Far from being outdated, templates are an example of a time-tested method that just keeps getting better.

Getting Ready

A template is an exact copy of a printed pattern. Patterns can be traced onto see-through materials like tissue paper (which must be glued onto more durable material) or transparent, heat-resistant plastic. Work in a well-lit area. Constructing templates, as well as marking and cutting fabric, requires precision; you must be able to see every marked line clearly. If you have trouble seeing the pattern through your template material, try a light box or a window on a sunny day. The light shining through the paper makes it easy to see the lines you are tracing.

A photocopier can also be used for duplicating patterns. However, check copies carefully for accuracy since some copiers have built-in distortion features.

What You'll Need

Fabric and craft scissors

Template plastic

Freezer paper

Ruler or straight edge

Fine-point permanent marking pen

Fine-point mechanical pencil, *or #2 or #3 pencil*

Colored quilt-marking pencils

Pencil sharpener

Rubber cement

Glue stick

Awl or ⅛" paper punch

Quilter's flexicurve (optional)

Light box (optional)

Step-by-Step Plastic Templates

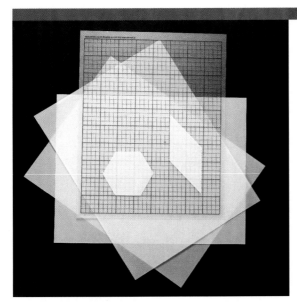

Traditionally, templates were made from lightweight cardboard or paper. Today's quilters prefer making templates from template plastic, which is a much more durable material that also retains an accurate shape and size. **Template plastic is available in a variety of thicknesses, and it can be transparent or opaque and plain or printed with a grid.** Some template plastic has a slightly rough surface to help keep templates from slipping on fabric. Experiment with different styles of template plastic to see which type works best for you.

Tip

Die-cut acrylic and metal templates are available commercially. They're great for hard-to-draft patterns and are extremely durable.

2

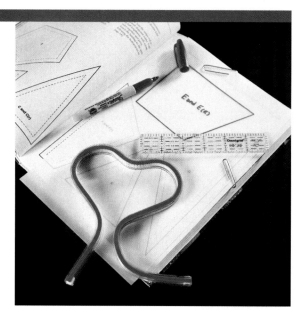

Place template plastic on top of the pattern and trace it with a fine-point permanent marking pen. To eliminate shifting, secure the plastic to the printed page with paper clips. If you have access to a photocopier, you may find it easier to work from a copy than from a book page. Make a full-size copy of the pattern, check it for accuracy, then tape it to your table. Tape the template plastic on top, and trace. A ruler helps keep straight lines wobble-free, and a flexible curve (a pliable edging guide available in quilt shops and art supply stores) serves the same purpose for tracing around curved shapes.

Always compare all finished templates with the original printed patterns to make sure they are a perfect match.

Tip

3

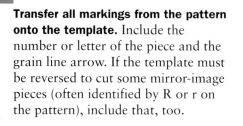

Transfer all markings from the pattern onto the template. Include the number or letter of the piece and the grain line arrow. If the template must be reversed to cut some mirror-image pieces (often identified by R or r on the pattern), include that, too.

4

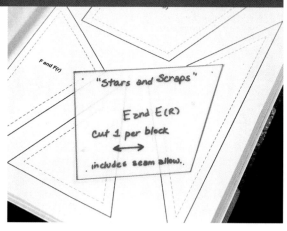

Hand-piecing templates represent the *finished* size of a patch, which is commonly shown as a dashed, inner line on printed patterns. Hand piecers mark the finished edge on the wrong side of the fabric so they know exactly where to stitch.

Machine-piecing templates represent the *unfinished* size of a patch. A ¼-inch seam allowance is included around the entire shape. **For machine-piecing templates, trace the outer, solid line of the printed pattern.** For either hand- or machine-piecing templates, cut out the templates with craft scissors *directly on the traced line.*

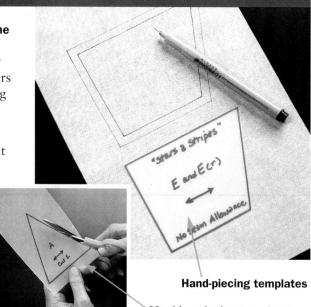

Hand-piecing templates

Machine-piecing templates

Always test new marking pens for permanence, and make sure ink doesn't bleed through the fabric and end up on the right side of your marked seams. Mechanical or very sharp pencils are good marking tools. For dark fabrics, try silver, white, or yellow lead. For lighter fabrics, try #2 or #3 lead, a red pencil, or a turquoise drafting pencil.

Tip

Keep your pencil sharp! A dull point makes a wider line that's further away from the actual size of the template.

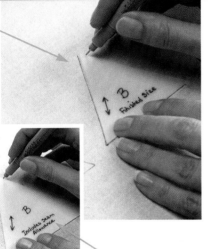

Hand-piecing templates

Machine-piecing templates

Tracing templates onto fabric is done similarly for both hand and machine piecing. Use a very sharp pencil or ultra-fine permanent marking pen, and trace around each template with the tip as close to the edge of the template as possible.

Hand Piecing: Trace templates *right side down* on the *wrong* side of the fabric. This prevents markings from showing on the finished patchwork. Leave at least ½ inch between marked patches for adding ¼-inch seam allowances by eye as you cut.

Machine Piecing: Trace templates *right side up* on the *right* side of the fabric. Cut out exactly on the line.

Tip

Layer fabric right sides together, trace your template, and cut both layers together to create a regular and reverse patch simultaneously.

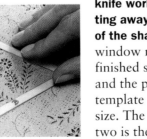

Window templates let you mark both seam *and* cutting lines with the same template, and they let you see exactly what part of the fabric will be featured in the finished quilt patch. **Transfer the entire pattern to template material, then cut on both the inner and outer lines. An X-Acto knife works well for cutting away the inner portion of the shape.** The inner window represents the finished size of the patch, and the perimeter of the template is the unfinished size. The area between the two is the seam allowance.

C U T T I N G   P A T C H E S   W I T H   T E M P L A T E S

Step-by-Step Freezer Paper Templates

1

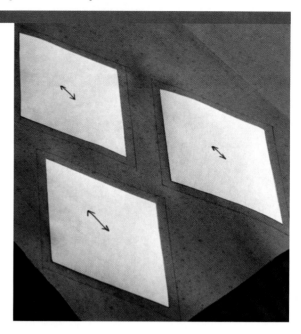

Freezer paper, the plastic-coated white paper used to wrap and freeze meat, is a handy tool for quilt-makers. Whether you buy it on a roll at the grocery store or select the gridded version available at quilt shops, it makes great templates. **Its waxy coating melts under the heat of an iron, adhering it to fabric where it acts as both a template and a stabilizer for stretchy fabrics like lightweight woven plaids and flannels.** It pulls off easily and can be reused several times before the coating will no longer hold. To make freezer paper templates, start by making one *plastic* template of each shape you need.

2

Tip

Freezer paper can be reused several times, so you may not need a separate template for each piece of the quilt.

Place a *finished*-size plastic template right side *down* on the nonwaxy side of freezer paper, and trace around it. Make a freezer paper piece for each patch in the block, and cut out directly on the lines. **Press the waxy side to the *wrong* side of fabric, leaving at least ½ inch between templates.**

3

Tip

You don't have to cut traced shapes for machine piecing with scissors. Align a rotary-cutting ruler on marked lines and slice!

Mark a ¼-inch seam allowance around each piece, then cut fabric on that line using scissors or a rotary cutter and ruler. Leave freezer paper on the patches until you sew them together. **Freezer paper works as a touchable guide that helps you align patches and shows you exactly where seams should begin and end.** The paper also stabilizes bias edges, which makes it easier to sew patches together without stretching.

The Quilter's Problem Solver

End Template Frustration

Problem	Solution
Fabric won't stay put when marking templates.	Use a rotary-cutting mat as a marking platform. Its nonskid surface grips fabric and holds it firmly as you trace around templates.
Templates slip on top of the fabric.	Apply a bit of rubber cement to the back of templates. Once dry, the gummy surface grips the fabric and keeps the template from slipping. Or, stick self-adhesive rubber or sandpaper dots to the back of your templates (look for these in hardware or home repair stores).
Fabric is printed off-grain, so stripes and other directional images are hard to align under the template.	Straighten the grain first by pulling gently on the fabric from corner to corner, along the bias. If the print is still off, align your template with the print, slightly off-grain if necessary. Remember to take extra care when handling those pieces.

Skill Builder

Cut patches off-grain on purpose to create special effects.

Selecting special areas of a printed fabric, such as a floral motif, doesn't always match the ideal grain placement. Don't sacrifice your design ideas; go ahead and cut the patch off-grain. Use a freezer paper template to stabilize it, or try a spritz of spray starch to keep edges ruly. Remember to handle it with care.

To cut patches, use a see-through plastic template, a window template, or use the first patch as an alignment tool to mark the rest. That way you'll be sure each patch is cut from the same design area of the fabric.

Try This!

When working with set-in pieces, use an awl or a ⅛-inch paper punch to **make holes in each template** where the seam lines intersect. Align the template on the wrong side of a fabric patch, poke a pencil through each hole, and mark the intersections. When you sew, the dots indicate exactly where each seam should end. Use the same technique to help you align other patches for sewing. For instance, mark seam-end dots on triangular pieces where sides must be offset for seams to match correctly. Or use dots as seam guides on hand-pieced patches, adding a few extra holes along the length of a seam.

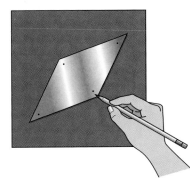

Rotary Cutting
for Precision Piecing

Rotary cutting has revolutionized quiltmaking—and with good reason. Rotary cutting eliminates tedious one-patch-at-a-time cutting. Triangles, one of the most commonly used shapes in quilts, are easy to mass produce using rotary short-cuts. Although rotary cutters have been most closely associated with template-free techniques, they can also be used with templates to cut tricky or odd-size shapes. Aside from speed, the other big benefit is highly accurate cutting, the foundation for perfect piecing.

Getting Ready

Do all rotary cutting on your rotary mat. Place it on a smooth surface and at a height that is comfortable for you to work at while standing. It's hard to get proper pressure and control of your rotary cutter or ruler when sitting.

Triangles are so quick and easy to prepare with rotary cutting that it's worthwhile to convert templates to rotary-cutting dimensions. Before cutting triangles, consider where you want the straight of grain to run. The rule of thumb is to have straight of grain on outside edges of blocks and quilt tops whenever possible. Half-square triangles have straight of grain along the two short sides, making them perfectly suited for corner setting triangles. Quarter-square triangles have straight of grain on the long sides, lending themselves to side setting triangles.

What You'll Need

Rotary cutter and mat

Rotary cutting rulers:

  6" × 24" *or* **6" × 12"**

  6" square

Prewashed, pressed fabric

Template plastic

Marking pencils

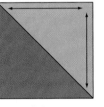

Half-Square Triangles   Quarter-Square Triangles

Step-by-Step Rotary-Cut Triangles

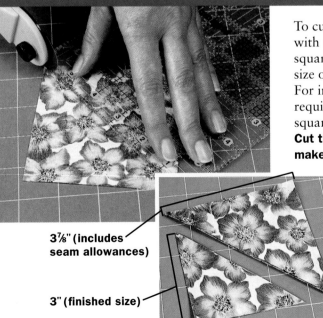

3⅞" (includes seam allowances)

3" (finished size)

To cut half-square triangles, start with a square. To calculate the size square, add ⅞ inch to the *finished* size of a short leg of the triangle. For instance, if your quilt pattern requires 3-inch finished triangle squares, start with 3⅞-inch squares. **Cut the square in half diagonally to make two triangles. Press down with your index finger on the ruler directly above the outer corner of the fabric square.** This added pressure prevents the corner of the square from moving as the cutter passes by. Triangles cut this way will have the straight of grain along the two short sides.

Tip

Layer light and dark fabric squares right sides together before cutting to make two pairs of triangles ready to sew together.

2

To cut quarter-square triangles with the straight of grain along the long edges, start with a square. Calculate the size square needed by adding 1¼ inches to the *finished size* of the long triangle edge. If the outer edge of patchwork needs to measure 3 inches finished, start with a 4¼-inch square.

Cut squares in half diagonally, as shown in Step 1 on page 25. Then, carefully lift your ruler and rotate the cutting mat so you can cut diagonally in the opposite direction.

Step-by-Step Converting Templates to Rotary Cutting

1

On an index card, draw the shapes and write the cutting dimensions inside each for easy reference.

Sometimes project directions provide only patterns for templates, with no rotary-cutting dimensions. **To convert from templates to rotary cutting, start by measuring the patterns.** As long as they have straight edges and dimensions are in increments of nothing smaller than eighths of an inch, you can cut patches with a rotary cutter and ruler.

If patterns don't include seam allowances, be sure to add them to get proper cutting dimensions. Add ½ inch to squares and rectangles for seam allowances. For half- and quarter-square triangles, follow the guidelines under "Step-by-Step Rotary Cut Triangles" on page 25. For diamonds, see Step 3.

2

Cut fabric strips to match one cutting dimension of your pattern piece. Then make additional cuts to get the shapes you need. For example, to get 3½-inch squares, cut a 3½-inch strip of fabric and subcut it into squares. For 4½ × 6½-inch rectangles, cut a 4½-inch strip and subcut into 6½-inch slices.

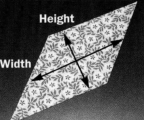

For diamonds, figure the cutting dimensions by adding ½ inch to the height and width of the diamond. Cut the strip to the same measurement as the height of the diamond. **Cut diamonds by aligning the 30, 45, or 60 degree line of your ruler with the bottom of the strip (choose the line that matches the angle of your particular pattern).** Make the first cut, then measure over from this cut the desired width of the diamond. Make the second cut to complete the diamond. Continue cutting diamonds from the strip in the same manner.

Tip

To test for accuracy, cut one piece first and measure against the printed pattern before cutting all pieces.

Step-by-Step Rotary Cutting with Templates

When patterns don't have exact ⅛-inch dimensions, or they have odd angles or more than four sides, make a plastic template for each shape you want to cut, including the seam allowance.

Mark around the template right side up on the right side of the fabric. For several of the same shape, layer up to four pieces of fabric, all right side up, with the marked fabric on top.

Refer to page 18 for making templates.

Tip

It's easiest and more accurate to mark just one layer of fabric, so mark first, then stack your fabrics.

Carefully align the edge of your rotary-cutting ruler with one of the marked lines, and cut. Rotate the ruler, line it up with the next line, and cut. Continue aligning and cutting until the patches are completely cut out. For quick and easy reverse (mirror image) pieces, stack the fabrics in pairs with right sides together. When the pieces are cut, you'll automatically have one reverse piece for each regular piece you cut. If you don't need reverse pieces, layer all fabrics right-side up.

The Perfect
¹/₄-Inch Seam

Being able to sew an exact ¹/₄-inch seam—every time—makes piecing easier and more enjoyable. In fact, if you've ever been frustrated in the past with ill-fitting pieces or out-of-square blocks one of the simple solutions in this lesson could be all you need to make the move to piecing perfection.

Getting Ready

Don't assume that because you have a ¼-inch patchwork foot or because your machine's throat plate has a ¼-inch marking that your seams are actually ¼ inch wide. It pays to test your finished seam allowance no matter what special equipment you have.

In fact, it's best to stitch a *scant* ¼-inch seam, because when pressing patchwork, some of the fabric tends to get taken up by the loft of the fold. Stitching the full ¼ inch, then pressing, takes up more fabric than intended, giving you patchwork that measures smaller than the desired finished size.

To test your seam allowance, start with fabric scraps that measure *exactly* 1 × 4 inches. And before you use graph paper for the test, double-check the size of the graph paper grid with a ¼-inch measurement on your rotary cutting ruler to be sure they are the same.

What You'll Need

- **Sewing machine**
- **Ruler with accurate ¼" markings**
- **¼" graph paper**
- **¼" masking tape**
- **Craft scissors**
- **Several 1" × 4" fabric pieces**
- **Fabric scissors *or* rotary-cutting supplies**
- **Iron and ironing board**
- **Dr. Scholl's moleskin (optional)**
- **¼" presser foot (optional, but recommended)**

Step-by-Step Accurate Seams

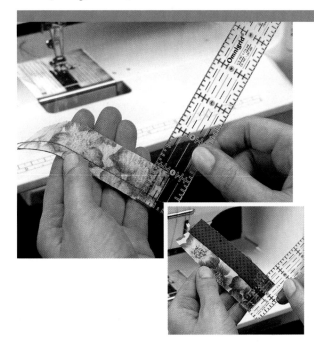

1

Sew two of the 1 × 4-inch fabric pieces together along the long edge using your normal ¼-inch seam. **Remove the fabric from the machine and measure the seam allowance with a rotary ruler.** Is it *exactly* ¼ inch? If it's exact or slightly wider than ¼ inch, your seam allowance is too wide and the finished patchwork will probably be too small. On the other hand, if it's much narrower than ¼ inch, the patchwork will be too big.

Press the patches open and measure their width. If the width of each strip measures exactly ¾ inch (for a total width of 1½ inches), your seam allowance is just where you want it to be. If not, continue on to Step 2.

Tip

If your machine has a changeable needle position, make sure it's in the center for testing the seam allowance.

To correct a too-wide or too-narrow seam allowance, cut a 2 × 4-inch rectangle from ¼-inch graph paper, cutting directly on the printed lines. **Position the paper with its long edge parallel to the raised presser foot. Lower the needle, piercing the paper just to the right of the first printed line from the right edge. Adjust the paper so the edge is parallel to the lines on the throat plate or presser foot.** With the needle still in the paper, lower the presser foot and tape the paper in place at the short ends. The right edge of the paper is now a scant ¼ inch from your needle.

3

Establish a handy seam guide by aligning a strip of masking tape with the paper's right edge. Position the strip as far as possible in front of the needle so that patches have a head start at the correct alignment. Make sure the tape doesn't extend over the feed dogs.

4

Tip

Self-adhesive, acrylic seam guides are available and can be used in place of tape. Some even include a feed dog notch.

If you have a ¼-inch presser foot, attach it to your machine. Does its right edge fit flush against the masking tape guide? If it does, you can remove the tape and use the foot to guide you (although a length of tape often helps in lining up fabrics accurately *before* they reach the needle). If it's slightly different, leave the tape in place and use it as your sewing guide.

If your sewing machine manufacturer does not offer a ¼-inch foot, try a Little Foot, available at quilt supply shops and in mail-order catalogs. (See page 11.)

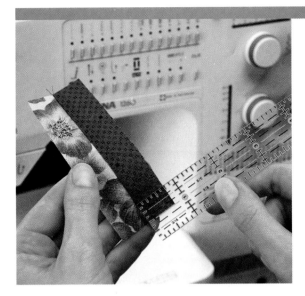

Now that the scant ¼-inch seam allowance is marked on your machine, remove the paper and do another sewing test, as described in Step 1. Open the sewn unit, pressing the seam allowance to one side. **Measure the strip widths. Remember, they should both measure exactly ¾ inch wide.** If your strips are off, adjust the seam guide and repeat the test until the strips are the correct width.

Tip

Your measuring will be more consistent if you always use the same brand of ruler, regardless of its size.

Once your seam allowance is accurate, build up the seam marker with layers of ¼-inch masking tape. The ridge of tape will keep your patches moving along accurately, with no chance of slipping to the side. Another option is to use a piece of Dr. Scholl's moleskin in place of the layers of tape. Moleskin is about ⅛ inch thick and is self-adhesive. **No matter which material you use, cut a notch in it to avoid covering the feed dogs.**

Tip

Masking tape and moleskin can wear away over time, especially if you sew a lot. Replace them periodically.

Some sewing machines have changeable needle positions, where the needle can move to the right or left of center. **If your machine has this feature, you may find that moving the needle to the right and doing the graph paper test from that needle position will let you mark your seam allowance along a groove in the throat plate.** A grooved line makes it easier to align masking tape so it's perfectly straight and parallel to the groove. If you change your needle position, however, you won't be able to use a ¼-inch foot. Remember to always set your needle to the same position before starting a patchwork project.

THE PERFECT ¼-INCH SEAM

Machine Piecing
Basics

*A*round *1865, when the mass marketing of the sewing machine swung into full gear, quilters suddenly had a choice—they could stitch by hand or by machine. Today, it's hard to imagine piecing without the wonderful benefits of the machine-powered needle. Machine piecing is fast, efficient, and strong. Plus, it offers shortcuts like assembly-line sewing and chain piecing to make quick work of repetitive steps. These fast and easy techniques not only streamline the patchwork process, but they can also improve accuracy.*

Getting Ready

Once you have decided on the pattern and selected your fabrics, you need to cut the fabric into the required shapes. Whether you cut your patches using templates or a rotary cutter, they'll need to have ¼-inch seam allowances on all sides, since you'll be matching the cut edges of the fabric pieces and stitching a (scant) ¼-inch seam allowance across the pieces from edge to edge.

If the pattern has set-in seams, it will be necessary to mark the seam corners ¼ inch from the edges of the fabric as starting and stopping points for sewing. We recommend reading "Setting in Seams with Ease" on page 76 before beginning.

See chapters on "Cutting Patches with Templates" (page 18), "Rotary Cutting for Precision Piecing" (page 24), and "The Perfect ¼-Inch Seam" (page 28) for more information on cutting fabric with appropriate seam allowances.

What You'll Need

- **Sewing machine**
- **Needles**
- **100% cotton sewing thread**
- **Cut pieces for patchwork block**
- **Silk pins**
- **Thread snips or embroidery scissors**
- **Seam ripper**
- **Iron and ironing board**
- **Stiletto or long pin**
- **Straight-stitch needle plate (optional, but recommended)**

Step-by-Step Traditional Machine Piecing

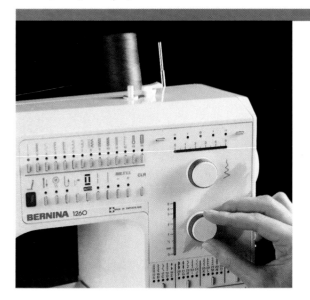

Get your machine ready for piecing. Insert a size 11 quilting needle or size 80/12 universal needle. If fabrics are similar in value (either dark or light) use matching thread for both top and bobbin. If the block has mixed values, use a darker neutral thread on top and a medium neutral shade in the bobbin. **Set the stitch length at 12 to 14 stitches per inch.** For European-made machines, this translates to a 2.0 to 2.5 stitch setting. Use a shorter stitch length (14 to 16 per inch, or 1.0 to 1.5) for seams that will be pressed open. (See "Pressing for Precision" on page 40.)

Tip

The thin shank of the size 11 quilting needle aids in accurate, consistent stitches.

MACHINE PIECING BASICS

2

Lay out the fabric pieces on your sewing table exactly as they will appear in the finished block or pattern you are constructing. This will help eliminate any confusion about which direction particular pieces need to be sewn together. Pay particular attention to fabrics that may have a directional print so that some are not vertical and others horizontal.

3

Pick up the first two patches to be joined, and place them with right sides together and cut edges aligned. Hold the edge that will be sewn so that it faces to the right to avoid confusion.

Tip

Since cotton naturally clings to itself, you may not need to pin straight-grain sewing edges. It's always good to pin bias.

4

Pin patches at the beginning and at the end of a seam line. Pin at the middle if necessary to hold the fabrics together securely. Pin across the seam allowances, positioning the pins so the heads are at the outside cut edge of the fabric for easy removal while sewing.

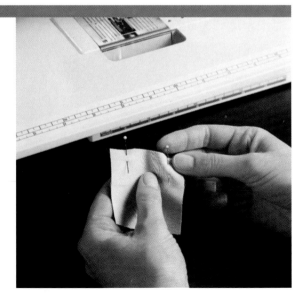

Place the pinned patches under the presser foot with the bulk of the fabric to the left. Begin stitching at the outer edge with the raw edges on the right aligned with your perfect ¼-inch seam marking. **Hold the ends of the top and bobbin threads in one hand so they don't get caught under the fabric as you sew the first few stitches.** Sew slowly, guiding the fabric along the ¼-inch marker. Don't pull, since that causes distortion.

It is not necessary to backstitch any seam that will be crossed by another line of machine stitching.

Remove pins just before you stitch over them. If you tempt fate and stitch over them, you risk bending or breaking a pin as well as your needle. Worse yet, you can throw off the timing of your machine, which can mean a costly visit to the sewing machine repair shop.

When you finish the seam, lift the presser foot, remove the piece, and **trim the beginning and ending threads.** If you are sewing triangles or other shapes that have dog ears, trim away the excess fabric, too. (See page 60 for information on trimming dog ears.)

Tip

Trim as needed after each step. If you wait until the block is complete, you risk snipping into adjoining patches.

MACHINE PIECING BASICS

Inspect the seam to make sure the ¼-inch seam allowance is even. If the line of stitching wobbles severely, you'll need to straighten it in order to maintain the accuracy of the block. **If the seam will be pressed to one side, it's possible to simply re-stitch a portion of the seam without ripping out the first set of stitches.**

9

Tip

It's often quicker and less frustrating to sew two new patches together than it is to rip out a bias-edge seam.

If the seam wobbled too far into the patch so that the seam allowance is wider than ¼-inch, you'll need to remove stitches. **To remove stitches quickly, slip a seam ripper slowly and carefully through the stitches on the bobbin side. Cut through every four to five stitches, then pull the top thread.**

10

Press or finger press the seam in the direction you have selected (see "Pressing for Precision" on page 40), and **replace the joined patches in your block layout.** Continue on, adding the third patch in the row, then repeat to piece the second and third rows.

Step-by-Step Speed Piecing

1

When constructing a block with identical parts, it saves time and thread to stitch similar units together in an assembly-line process. The pieces sewn with chain piecing will be more accurate as a result of the consistency achieved by sewing the same unit repeatedly. Select pairs of patches that are identical. Pin them together, being careful to keep the same fabric on top. **Stack the pairs on one side of the machine, with the same edge facing right, ready to be picked up in turn.**

2

To stabilize the initial stitches on the first patch, use a "scrap starter." **Stitch across a double thickness of a small piece of scrap fabric, stopping at the edge, keeping the fabric under the presser foot.** Position the first pair of patches so they are butted directly against the last edge of the scrap starter, so that the next stitches will be sewn on the patches.

Remember to always pick up the patches so the same fabric is on top and the same edge is going under the needle.

3

Continue butting the pairs of patches, each one against the last edge of the previous one, and stitching across to the edge. Be careful that you don't overlap them. When you stop sewing to pick up the next patches, make sure the needle is down in the fabric to prevent the pieces from slipping out of alignment.

If you have a needle down feature on your machine, use it to make chain piecing even more effortless.

MACHINE PIECING BASICS

4

If the pairs of patches involve points and tips, as with triangles, it may be necessary to hold those points flat as they approach the needle. **Use a long pin or stiletto to hold the fabric tips so they won't be pulled into the needle hole of the sewing machine.**

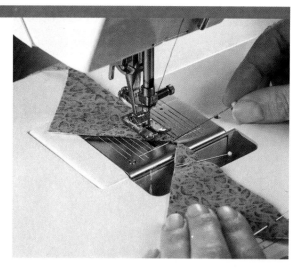

5

When the line of chained pieces is completed, clip them apart. If there are tips of triangles sticking out beyond the seam edges, trim them as you go, for efficient use of your time. Trimming the triangle tips or dog ears before pressing them will also lessen your chance of stretching the finished unit as you press. Trim one set of dog ears first and check the trimming angle for accuracy before trimming all dog ears.

6

In some cases, it is feasible to sew chained units to other units to complete a block without clipping them apart first. Chain sew larger units together, just as you did two individual patches. **In this Nine Patch block example, the rows were chain stitched together. Without clipping the connecting threads, turn the block, pin, and sew the crosswise seams.** The connecting chain stitching ensures your patches will go together in the correct order. There's no confusion over which row goes where.

PERFECT PIECING

The Quilter's
Problem Solver

Piecing Inconsistencies

Problem	Solution
Stitches are inconsistent or wobbly.	First, check that your machine and bobbin are threaded correctly. Next, check the needle. Is it inserted properly? Is it dull or burred? As a last resort, check the machine tension.
Patches aren't the right size after being sewn.	The problem could be caused by one of three things. To determine which problem you are having: (1) Measure your cut patches. Are they exactly the size they should be? (2) Check your $\frac{1}{4}$-inch seam allowance, and see "The Perfect $\frac{1}{4}$-Inch Seam" on page 28 for ways to ensure that your seam allowance is accurate. (3) Check your pressing. If your sewing is accurate but your patches are still off, improper pressing could be the cause. See "Pressing for Precision" on page 40.
Seams tend to be jerky because my foot pedal keeps moving as I sew.	A computer mouse pad prevents your foot pedal from traveling across the floor or carpet.

Skill Builder

Use these simple tricks to make piecing easier.

❏ Concentrate on the cut edges of the fabrics as they pass under the presser foot—not the needle—to make sure you are sewing at ¼ inch.

❏ If a seam is longer than 2 or 3 inches, pin along the seam—not just the beginning and the end—to stabilize the two fabrics.

❏ When sewing angled, pointed pieces, begin stitching at the wide end of the patch so the skinny point won't disappear into the feed dogs.

Try This!

As you piece a block, keep it laid out as it will appear when finished, laying the pieced patches back in place at each step. If you are chain piecing several units, after they are clipped apart, position them in the pattern, too. It's incredibly easy to pick up the wrong patches or to sew the wrong edges together, creating a new design without intending to!

Pressing
for Precision

Proper pressing is an essential part of precise piecing. Units fit together more easily and accurately when the bulk created by the seams is flattened, and finished blocks look neat and crisp when pressed smooth. But, while pressing is important, it's also possible to overdo it and distort your piecing. Fortunately, it takes just a couple of tricks to master perfect pressing.

Getting Ready

Situate your pressing area as close as possible to your sewing setup. When buying an iron, choose the best you can afford. Make sure it's comfortable and not too heavy to handle. After all, it's the heat, not the weight, that is most important.

Use a dry setting for pressing seams. Steam flattens seams more effectively, making a very sharp crease at the seam line, but it's difficult to undo if you change your mind about which direction the seam should lie. Steam also dampens the fabric, making it stretch and distort more easily. Reserve steam for the final blocking of the piece.

Make a pressing plan before beginning to sew. It's much easier to match seam intersections in your quilt blocks when seams are pressed in opposite directions. So think about the order you'll be piecing in and how pressing the seam will affect the next part of your piecing.

Step-by-Step Pressing for Precision

1

Ironing involves a back-and-forth motion that can push grain lines out of square and cause patches to be misshapen and distorted. **In quilt-making you should *press*, lifting and placing the iron on the surface of the pieced fabric repeatedly.** Each time you move to a new area of the fabric, lift the iron first. Don't glide it across the surface. The iron should only be moved in the direction of the fabric grain—not at an angle—to avoid distortion.

PRESSING FOR PRECISION

2

Before pressing the seam allowances in any direction, "set" the seam by pressing directly on the line of stitching before opening the patches. This relaxes the thread and imbeds the stitches into the fabric. In addition, it smoothes any slight fullness and produces a flatter seam when the pieces of fabric are opened.

3

Traditionally, quilt seams are pressed to one side. The seam is stronger because any stress at the seam line is borne by the fabric, not just the joining stitches. In addition, batting won't be able to puff out between the stitches. These considerations are especially important with hand-pieced seams since the stitches aren't as secure as those stitched by machine.

4

Seam pressed in the wrong direction? Correct it by pressing it flat, as for setting stitches. Then press in the opposite direction.

In addition, by pressing the seams to one side you can use the bulk of the seam allowances to help you match seam intersections, and this may be the best reason of all for pressing to one side. Plan ahead and press seams for pieces that will be joined together in opposite directions.

Shadow-through, the shading of a dark color through a lighter one, detracts from the look of a seam and can be avoided by pressing the seam allowances toward the darker piece. **Place the sewn unit on the ironing board with the dark fabric on top and the seam allowance facing away from you. When the patches are opened, the seam will automatically be pressed toward the dark fabric.**

Sometimes it is necessary to press the seam allowance toward the lighter piece to reduce excess bulk. **However, to avoid shadow-through, you'll need to grade the seam allowances so that the lighter one is larger, overlapping the darker one.**

Tip

When grading seam allowances, remember they're only ¼" to start with, so trim off as little as possible.

For blocks that have many thicknesses of fabric joining together, pressing seams to one side can create a wad of fabric that can "roll" and distort precise matches. These seams can be pressed open, as long as the stitches are small enough (14 to 16 per inch) to produce a strong seam.

Pressing the seam allowances open is time-consuming and, since the seam allowance is a scant ¼ inch, it is easy to burn your fingertips. Open and flatten the seam allowance with your fingers before using the iron, **then use a stiletto, long pin, awl, or the tip of your seam ripper to hold the fabrics open as you advance the iron.**

Tip

Press the seam open from the wrong side and then from the right side to ensure it is flat.

Never sew over an unpressed seam. Both hand- and machine-pieced units will fit together more smoothly and accurately if the seams are pressed before they are sewn over. In place of an iron, you can finger press a seam. **Use your fingernail, the flat side of a closed pair of scissors, or a Little Wooden Iron if a standard iron is not available.**

PRESSING FOR PRECISION

Step-by-Step Pressing for Completed Blocks

1

Tip

Keep your iron and sewing machine plugged into the same surge protector strip for quick, one-button on and off.

Check the block to make sure you have turned the seam allowances in the directions you intended. If you have changed your mind about any seams, correct them with a dry iron.

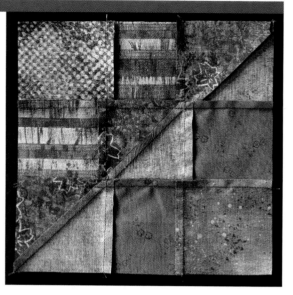

2

It's not unusual for blocks to vary slightly in size, by ⅛ to ¼ inch, or so. By blocking them to the same size with steam, you'll have a much easier time assembling them into a quilt top.

If you don't have a gridded ironing board cover, draw a blocking line on your ironing board cover or on a piece of muslin with a permanent marker. Use a rotary ruler to make sure your drawn block is perfectly square and accurate. A 15-inch square ruler works well for this step. **If you are drawing on a large muslin square, pin it securely in place on the ironing board cover.**

3

Pin the block in place, right side up, stretching it slightly if necessary, so that the block edges align with the drawn guide. Make sure all corners align. If necessary, pin each corner in place with a straight pin. **Then, steam press the block, using the iron to manipulate block edges to align with the drawn guidelines.** Be sure to press only with the grain and do not move the block until it has cooled.

The Quilter's
Problem Solver

Pressing Predicaments

Problem	Solution
Small pleats close to the seam on the front of the block.	Press the seam allowance in the chosen direction, lightly from the wrong side, then firmly from the top side. Press out from the seam in the direction of the grainline.
Seam allowances show through the top, sometimes as a shiny lump.	Set the seams firmly before pressing them. Trim away excess bulk where possible. Place a piece of fabric (or paper towel) between the top fabric and the seam allowance before you press.
Where seams join, block appears lumpy.	Fan bulky seam allowances at intersections with multiple points, such as the center of an eight-pointed star, to reduce bulk. (See page 84.)
Blocks aren't all consistent size.	To assist in blocking, spray mist your block with water for the final pressing.

Skill Builder

Plan pressing before you begin to stitch.

While pressing toward the darker fabric prevents show-through, there may be other considerations:

❑ **Multiple joins**—for easier piecing, press seam allowances of the two units in opposite directions at the joining points.

❑ **Quilting in the ditch**—press the seam allowances *away* from the background.

❑ **Point areas**—*grade* the seam allowances sharply so that they'll fold into the space.

Try This!

When traveling to quilting classes, or even at home, **it's nice to have an ironing area close at hand.** Cover a cardboard core from a used-up bolt of fabric (free from your favorite quilt shop) with a layer of thin batting followed by a muslin or flannel remnant. It makes a fine lightweight ironing board to have at your elbow near the sewing machine. It can lay on a cabinet or across an open drawer. And it's easy to transport. Heat-resistant ironing board cover fabric is also available, if desired.

Matching Magic for
Individual Pieces

PERFECT PIECING

Aligning same-size and same-shape patches for sewing is easy. But when the pieces have different shapes, matching gets a little trickier. Triangle and diamond points extend beyond the edges of squares, making it look as if at least one of the pieces were cut wrong. Worse yet, matching two different-shaped triangles for stitching can be totally baffling. Our tips take the guesswork out of aligning even the trickiest shapes and angles.

Getting Ready

Squares and right triangles are used frequently by quiltmakers, and after sewing a few together you become accustomed to how the patches need to align for a perfectly matched seam. Other shapes are used less often, so matching them accurately by eye doesn't become second nature for most of us. For these cases, make a trimming template to snip away excess dog ears or points. With the points trimmed off, patches can be matched with ease. Even if you prefer rotary cutting for diamonds and trapezoids, make a plastic template of each shape that includes seam allowances. Step 6 on page 49 shows you how to transform that into a trimming template.

What You'll Need

Cut pieces for patchwork block

Silk pins

Sewing machine

100% cotton sewing thread

Thread snips or embroidery scissors

Template plastic

Marking pen or pencil

See-through ruler

Craft scissors

Step-by-Step Matching Pieces

¼"

When you need to match the short side of a right triangle to the edge of a square or rectangle, you'll notice that the triangle edge is longer than that of the square. **Align the pieces so the edges match at one corner of the square. The tips of the triangle will extend beyond two corners of the square. Pin the two patches together.** The triangle point should intersect the square exactly ¼ inch from the side of the square.

After stitching and pressing the seam to one side, **trim off the extending triangle points** to reduce bulk in the finished quilt.

Tip

When attaching triangles to each side of a square, sew the first two triangles on opposite sides; then add the remaining triangles.

Sometimes the long edge of a right triangle is sewn to the side of a square. The long triangle edge will be longer than the square, with the tips extending past both ends of the square. **To make matching easy, fold the square in half and crease to mark the midpoint. Repeat with the triangle, folding the long edge in half. Align the edges, matching the finger-pressed creases.**

Without stretching the bias edge of the triangle, pin the two patches together and stitch from edge to edge. Press and trim the points, as described in Step 1 on page 47.

Diamonds (or any parallelogram) are cut on an angle, which means they'll often have tips that extend beyond the edges of other patches. Diamonds have two different angles; a narrow one at the pointy ends, and a wider one at the two other corners.

Sewing diamonds to squares or rectangles usually includes set-in seams.

Refer to page 52 for complete details on using matching points for this type of seam.

Sewing diamonds to triangles, on the other hand, is a lot easier. **The triangle and diamond are cut at the same angle, so matching them is just like matching the edges of two right triangles. Align the long diagonal cut of the triangle with the same length edge of the diamond.** Pin and stitch, taking care not to stretch the bias cut edges.

Many popular star blocks, such as 54-40 or Fight, contain long, skinny points. These are formed by joining two long, thin right triangles to an isosceles triangle (one with two equal-length sides and no right angles). **When the seams for these pieces are aligned properly for stitching, dog ears will extend in all directions—some thin, some fat.** The easiest way to take the guesswork out of matching different triangle shapes is to create a trimming template. This handy tool is used to trim away the excess fabric (dog ears) before aligning the patches, so all sides of the triangles can be positioned accurately.

Start with your plastic templates that were discussed in "Getting Ready" on page 47. These should include seam allowances. Use a see-through ruler and marking pen or pencil to draw the seam line on both templates. **Then overlay the templates so the seam intersections match.** Tape the templates together so they don't shift.

Notice how the tips of each triangle template extend beyond the edge of the other template. **Use your rotary cutter or craft scissors to trim away the points on both templates.**

Tip

Have an extra rotary cutter? Keep an old blade in one and use it just for cutting template plastic.

After rotary cutting fabric triangles, lay your trimming template over the patch, aligning the sides. The tips of the fabric will extend beyond the end of the template. Mark along the edge of the template to trim off the dog ears with scissors. Or, lay a rotary-cutting ruler on top of the template and trim with your rotary cutter.

Now align the patches for sewing. The tips are cut at exactly the same angles, so there's no guesswork about how to line them up for an accurate seam and a square block.

Matching Magic for
Seam Intersections

A perfectly matched seam is a beauty to behold. From a simple four patch to a more ambitious Feathered Star, any block you make is enhanced by seams that intersect exactly where they should. And even beyond the internal piecing of a block, accurately matched seams between blocks, sashings, and borders help create a quilt that's square and true.

Getting Ready

Precise cutting, accurate stitching, and careful pressing all contribute to well-matched seam intersections. Inaccuracy in any of these areas can lead to problems when it comes to matching points and seam intersections. If you have doubts about your proficiency in any of these areas, you may find it helpful to refer to the following chapters for guidance.

See "Cutting Patches with Templates" on page 18, "Rotary Cutting for Precision Piecing" on page 24, "The Perfect ¼-Inch Seam" on page 28, and "Pressing for Precision" on page.

What You'll Need

Pressed pieces and/or quilt blocks

Silk pins

Sewing machine

100% cotton sewing thread

Stiletto or seam ripper

Scissors or thread snips

Ruler

Step-by-Step Simple Cross Seams

The simplest matching involves butting perpendicular seams. **Hold the two units together, snugging the seam allowances together until you feel that the seams match exactly. Pin on either side of this seam intersection, placing the pins perpendicular to the fabric edge.** The pins hold the seam in place as well as keep the seam allowances from flipping up as you stitch the seam.

2

Stitch the seam, removing the pins as you approach them. **If possible, stitch with the seam allowance of the piece underneath facing you and the seam allowance of the top piece away from you.** That way, you can keep the top

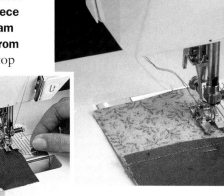

seam allowance from folding under with a straight pin or a stiletto, and the feed dogs will control the seam allowance on the piece underneath.

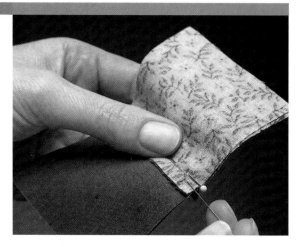

Tip

Roll back the edges before pinning to make sure cross seams match where the seam will be sewn— ¼" below the raw edge.

3

Sometimes, it's just not possible to have seams pressed in opposite directions. To match seams that are pressed in the same direction, it is especially important to press the seams firmly and pin the intersection securely, to avoid the matching point being pushed out of alignment. First, pin directly along the side of the seam without seam allowances, to hold the matched seam intersection in position. **Then pin through the bulk of the double seam allowances.**

Step-by-Step Matching Diagonal and Multiple Seams

1

Some matches involve several different seams coming together. In these situations, it's more difficult to feel where the center match point should be. Don't rely just on feel. **Roll the edges back so you can see ¼ inch below the cut edges of the fabric.** The match point may have several stitching lines coming through it, but it's at this point— ¼ inch below the raw edges—that the seam intersections need to match. **Stab a pin vertically through the center match point, holding the top and bottom pieces together.** Keep this pin standing upright in the fabrics; don't pin it down or you may skew the perfect match.

Tip

Press seam allowances open at intersections with multiple lines or points to make matching easier.

Pin on either side of the first pin to hold the fabrics together firmly so the matched joining area doesn't shift. Stitch, holding the stabbed pin steady to keep it vertical, removing it and the stabilizing pins as they near the needle.

No matter how careful you are when pinning seam intersections, sometimes you'll sew an intersection that doesn't match when pressed open. **In this case, rip stitches ½ inch to 1 inch on each side of the intersection point.** Repin, and sew from the opposite direction.

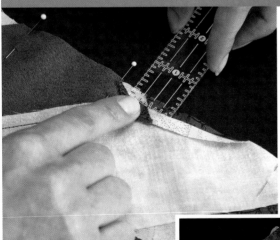

Because of the angle of the matched pieces, some simple intersections must be offset and matched not at the cut edge of the fabric, but at points ¼ inch inside the seam allowance. The seam allowances angle away from each other and cannot be used to judge the match. **So, in addition to stab pinning, roll these seam allowances back, as in Step 1 on the opposite page, to check the exact matching points. Because these are diagonal seams, not multiple seams, it's harder to judge where the seam intersection should be. A small ruler comes in handy to measure the ¼-inch distance.** Pinch the fabric together and pin securely. Again, use the feed dogs to your advantage and sew with the top seam allowance facing away from you.

Tip

Tip

With a complex intersection, you may wish to keep the fabric tightly pinned. It is possible to stitch over the stabilizing pins, but you must sew *slowly*.

Tip

Baste across complex intersections by hand or machine before stitching to make sure all angles and points are aligned.

MATCHING SEAM INTERSECTIONS

Time-Saving
Strip Piecing

Strip piecing is like the microwave of quiltmaking—it's an easy shortcut that makes you wonder how you ever lived without it. In this technique, long strips of fabric are cut, sewn, and pressed to create strip sets, which are then sliced into ready-made rows or shapes for quilt blocks or patterns. No matter how you slice it, strip piecing is fast, easy, and promotes accuracy. What more could any quilter ask for?

Getting Ready

Many blocks and quilts—both traditional and contemporary—can be constructed entirely with strip piecing. Others use this technique for sections of the design. To analyze blocks for strip piecing, look for rows of rectangles, as in Rail Fence; checkerboard squares, as in Nine Patch; or strips cut into shapes, as in Roman Stripe. More intricate patterns that use the same shape, such as the diamonds in Lone Star, can be strip-pieced using multiple strip sets in different color sequences.

Cut strips the width of the *unfinished* patches. For example, if a pattern calls for cutting 3½-inch squares that will finish at 3 inches, cut strips 3½ inches wide. Cut strips across the fabric width unless the direction of a print dictates otherwise. Strips can be marked and then cut with scissors, but a rotary cutter makes this task a quick and easy one.

What You'll Need

Pattern adapted for strip piecing, such as Nine Patch

Two or more fabrics

Rotary-cutting supplies

Silk pins

Iron and ironing board

Sewing machine

100% cotton sewing thread

Thread snips or embroidery scissors

Template plastic

Craft scissors

Rail Fence

Nine Patch

Roman Stripe

Step-by-Step Strip Piecing

1

·Align two strips right sides together, matching the cut edges. **Pressing the strips together helps hold them firmly in place while sewing, or you can also pin the strips along the cut edge to hold them securely.**

Tip

If your strip lengths vary, match the short end where you start sewing and don't worry about the other ends.

2

Tip

Stitches will be cut repeatedly when you slice segments, so sew with tighter stitches (14 to 16 per inch).

Stitch slowly, keeping your eye on the ¼-inch mark, not on the needle. It is especially important to stitch with a consistent seam allowance with this technique, since your seams will be 40 or more inches long.

3

Tip

Start pressing strips open at the center and work out to the ends to avoid "warping."

Press toward the darker strip unless pattern directions state otherwise. For wider strips, lay the unopened strip set on the ironing board with the darker fabric on top and the seam allowances facing away from you. Press to set the seam. **Then open the strip set and press. The seam will automatically be pushed toward the dark strip.**
For narrow strips, open up the strip set and press lightly from the wrong side. Then press firmly from the right side.

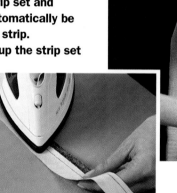

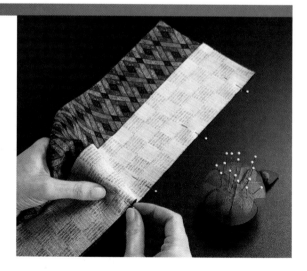

4

If there are more than two strips in the set, add the next strip, aligning the cut edges and pinning as before. Always begin stitching from the same end of a strip set, to reduce curving and distorting the long seam.

Press each new seam before adding another strip to keep the strip set flat. **Generally, all seams are pressed in the same direction. However, for patterns with an odd number of strips and strong color contrast, you can press the seams into or away from a center strip, depending on whether the center strip is the dark or light fabric.** This controls seam allowance shadow-through and allows for butted seams in the final block assembly.

Multiple-strip sets tend to be wavy, due to all the long seams. Hold the seams straight and block the strip set by giving a final press with steam. Let the strip set dry before cutting.

Cut across the strip set, either perpendicularly or at an angle (as required by your pattern) to trim off the selvage ends and square up the edge. Use the width of the strips cut for the strip set as your cutting measurement and slice off a segment. This produces one completed row for your block or design. For instance, if you cut 2½-inch strips for a strip set to make a Nine Patch block, cut 2½-inch-wide segments from the sewn strip set. **For a Lone Star, cut diagonal segments using the 45 degree marking on the ruler.**

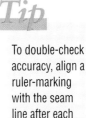

Tip

To double-check accuracy, align a ruler-marking with the seam line after each cut. Recut ends of strips, as necessary.

To cut a shape from the strip set, draw and cut around a template, or use the angled lines on a ruler and cut with the rotary cutter. Be sure to orient the shape squarely with the seam lines of the strip set so your stripes aren't askew in the finished block. If you use a rotary cutter to cut shapes, it's more accurate to align a ruler marking with one of the seam lines, instead of the outer edges of the strip set.

TIME-SAVING STRIP PIECING

Individual
Triangle Squares

I n the world of quilt designs, triangle squares are everywhere. Over the years,
quiltmakers have used these versatile squares in every combination imaginable to
create an endless variety of patterns. Two quick and easy ways to make triangle
squares, the Slice-and-Sew and the Layered-Squares methods, are described in this chapter.

Getting Ready

This chapter focuses on two ways to make individual triangle squares—the Slice-and-Sew method and the Layered-Squares method. Both techniques are good when you want a scrappy look because they give you the opportunity to make use of small pieces of fabric. If you need a great number of *identical* triangle squares, see "Grid-Method Triangle Squares" on page 64 and "Bias-Square Triangles" on page 68 before you begin, for information on quick piecing techniques that might be more suitable for your project.

Whichever method you choose, you need to know one little formula before you cut your pieces: Always add ⅞ inch to the *finished size* of the triangle square to determine the *cutting size*. For example, if you need triangle squares that finish at 3 inches, cut triangles that measure 3⅞ inches on the short sides.

 See "The Perfect ¼-Inch Seam" on page 28 before beginning to make sure your machine is set up to sew an accurate ¼-inch seam allowance.

What You'll Need

Two or more fabrics (scraps are fine)

Rotary-cutting supplies (a 6" square ruler works great) or template material and scissors

Sewing machine

100% cotton sewing thread

Iron and ironing board

Pencil or permanent marking pen

Spray starch or sizing (optional)

Step-by-Step Slice-and-Sew Method

1

3⅞"

Sewing two right triangles together is the most basic method for making triangle squares. To cut out the right triangles you could use a template, or simply **cut a square on the fabric's straight of grain with your rotary cutting equipment. Then cut the square in half diagonally.** Remember, the size of your square needs to be ⅞ inch larger than your desired finished size triangle square. Cut the same size triangles from two different fabrics for each triangle square.

Tip

Handle triangles carefully to avoid stretching their long bias edges.

2

Carefully align the edges of two triangles, right sides together. Use a ¼-inch seam allowance and sew triangles together along their longest side. **If triangle tips tend to slide apart or pull to one side as they approach the needle, pin to keep them aligned. Use the pin as a handle to guide the tips so you can maintain an accurate seam allowance.**

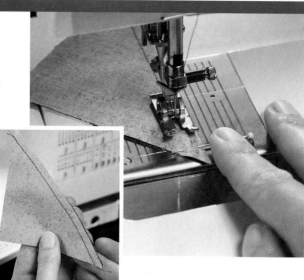

If you're making more than one triangle square, chain piece them, as shown on page 37. You'll avoid chewed triangle tips and save time and thread, too.

3

Whenever possible, press the seam allowance toward the darkest fabric. Pressing in this direction helps to mask shadows that might show through on the front of the finished piece. **Place the triangle square on your ironing board dark side up, and press it flat to set the seam.**

Flip open the dark triangle, using your fingers to _gently_ push it away from the center seam. Bring the iron straight down on top of the unit to press it open. Don't move the iron back and forth—triangle squares stretch easily.

4

After the triangle square is pressed open, you'll see the extra seam allowance at the triangle tips, often called dog ears. **Use scissors or rotary-cutting equipment to trim the tips flush with the sides of the square.** This eliminates unwanted bulk as you piece the triangle squares into your quilt block.

If you're using rotary-cutting equipment, you can double-check your triangle square for accuracy at the same time. If you started out with 3⅞-inch triangles, the triangle square should measure 3½ inches square.

Step-by-Step Layered-Squares Method

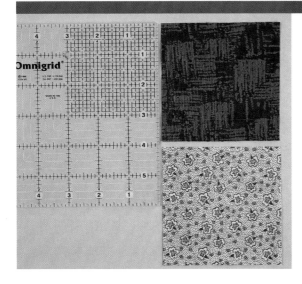

If you need at least two same-size triangle squares that contain the same two fabrics, try this quick-piecing method that eliminates handling cut bias edges. **Cut two squares, each ⅞ inch bigger than the desired finished-size triangle square.**

Layer two squares right sides together. **Use a pencil or fine-point permanent marker to draw a diagonal line from corner to corner on the wrong side of the lighter square.** Choose a pencil or marker that doesn't drag and pull on the fabric. You're marking along the bias and don't want to stretch it out of shape. If you spritz the squares with spray starch and press them before marking, the squares will hug together, and the starch will help any pencil or marker flow more easily.

Tip

Don't use a ballpoint pen to mark your fabric. The ink may smear or bleed.

Align the ¼-inch line of a rotary ruler a hair to the left of your drawn line, and draw a second diagonal line ¼ inch to the right of the original line. This is a stitching line that will produce a scant ¼-inch seam allowance. Repeat on the other side of the original diagonal line. If you have a ¼-inch presser foot, you can omit drawing the stitching lines.

Tip

A small rotary mat, with its no-skid texture, is perfect for holding fabric in place so you can draw accurate lines.

4

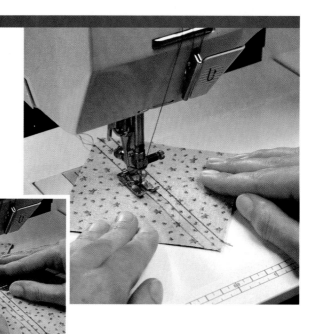

Tip

Sew in the same direction on each side of the center diagonal to avoid stretching or twisting your fabric.

Position light and dark squares *right sides* together. **Sew along both marked seam lines** (or use your ¼-inch presser foot to sew a seam on each side of the diagonal line).

For faster assembly, prepare several squares for sewing, chain piece to sew one seam on each pair, and chain piece again to complete the second seam. You don't even have to clip the chained pieces apart before sewing the second row. You can clip both rows of stitching at one time after all sewing is complete.

5

Press to set stitches. **Align the edge of your rotary ruler with the original, marked line, and cut the square in half.** (Scissors can be used, if you prefer.) Refer to Steps 3 and 4 under the "Step-by-Step Slice-and-Sew" method on page 60 for pressing and trimming directions.

6

Each set of squares yields two pairs of identical triangle squares.

Use scissors or a rotary cutter to trim the dog ears, as shown in Step 4 on page 60.

The Quilter's
Problem Solver

Inaccurate Triangle Squares

Problem	Solution
Triangle squares are smaller than they should be.	Try a scant ¼-inch seam allowance. Also check that the seam is pressed all the way open, without a lip or crease of extra fabric.
Triangle squares are distorted, not square.	If your seam allowances are accurate and consistent, the problem could be improper pressing. It's easy to get a bit heavy-handed with the iron, but don't move it back and forth across a patch. Instead, bring it down directly on the area to be pressed, without any side-to-side motion. Steam, too, can add to the distortion. Try a dry iron.
Finished triangle squares tend to stretch easily.	The short sides of triangles must be aligned as close as possible to the straight of grain, or you'll end up with somewhat of a bias edge on all sides of your triangle square. If you can't see the grain on the front side of fabric because of the print, try viewing it from the back.

Skill Builder

Cut and mark triangle squares accurately with these pro pointers.

❏ To avoid stretching when marking squares along the bias, don't start at a corner. Begin at the midpoint and mark outward. Return to the midpoint to finish marking the line.

❏ For perfect triangle squares (especially very small ones), cut triangles or squares slightly larger than necessary. If you need 3-inch finished triangle squares, cut your fabric squares 4 inches instead of 3⅞ inches. After sewing and pressing, trim the triangle square to the exact size required. Remember to leave ¼-inch seam allowances, so in our example, you'd trim to 3½ inches.

Try This!

Keep a **Quilter's Quarter** next to your sewing machine. This see-through plastic "stick" measures ¼ inch on each side of its center line, making it handy for marking and checking seams. To mark for the layered-squares method, align the center groove so it diagonally intersects two corners of your square. Mark a line in the center groove and on each side. Marking couldn't be easier.

To use it for checking seam allowances, simply align the center slot with the stitching. The edge should align with the raw edge of your fabric.

INDIVIDUAL TRIANGLE SQUARES

Grid-Method
Triangle Squares

I t's a quilter's dream come true! Here's a way to make perfectly matched triangle squares quickly and easily without cutting and stitching individual triangles. With the grid method there are no templates to make, and you won't have to worry about stretching the bias edge of the triangles. All it takes is a little simple math and one session at the sewing machine and you can make as many identical triangle squares as you need, enjoying the dual benefits of mass production and pinpoint accuracy!

Getting Ready

Determine how many triangle squares you'll need and divide that number by two (each square in the grid makes two triangle squares when sewn and cut apart). Next, determine the *finished* size of the squares you need. Add ⅞ inch to the finished size for seam allowances. For instance, if you need a triangle square that finishes at 3 inches for your block, start with a 3⅞-inch square grid. For a 4½-inch finished square, you'll need a 5⅜-inch grid.

Next figure out how much fabric you need. Here's an example: If you need 32 triangle squares that are 3 inches finished, you need a grid with 16 squares (32 ÷ 2 = 16). A grid of 4 squares by 4 squares will measure 15½ inches square (4 squares × 3⅞). This grid easily fits on a fat quarter of fabric (18 × 22 inches) with room to spare.

Step-by-Step Grid Method

1

Layer the two fabrics right sides together, with the lighter fabric on top. Spray with starch or sizing and press dry. The starch gives a firmer surface for drawing the grid and makes stitching easier, too, since fabric won't easily be pulled into the stitch plate.

2

Use your rotary ruler to draw lines on the light fabric. After drawing the first line about 1 inch or so from the edge of the fabric, measure over the distance of your grid and draw the next line. Continue until all lines are drawn in one direction. Keep the pencil sharp or use a mechanical one. Hold it at an angle so the point is tight against the ruler.

If you find it difficult to draw on the fabric, draw the grid on tissue paper. Pin the paper through both layers of fabric and sew 14 to 16 stitches per inch. Tear away paper when all stitching and cutting is completed.

3

Turn the fabric a quarter turn and repeat the process of drawing lines, as explained in Step 2. Double-check that the squares are all the same size.

Draw diagonal lines through each square, following the pattern shown in Step 4. To accurately mark the diagonal lines, hold the ruler so that it just misses intersecting the horizontal and vertical lines. This will let your *pencil point* be the tool that actually does the intersecting.

4

If you do not have an accurate ¼-inch presser foot, draw lines ¼ inch from both sides of the diagonal lines to serve as stitching lines. **These are indicated by the dashed lines in the illustration.** Again, check the ruler position to make sure the new lines are exactly ¼ inch from the first diagonal lines.

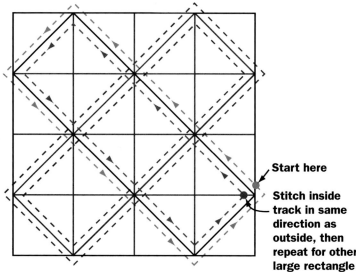

Start here

Stitch inside track in same direction as outside, then repeat for other large rectangle

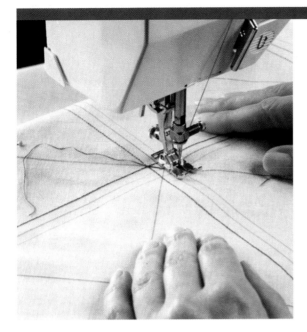

Pin the layers together, keeping pins away from the stitching lines. **Stitch ¼ inch on both sides of the diagonal lines, sewing with 12 to 14 stitches per inch.** Sew as far as you can along one line before moving to the next one, following the stitching order shown in Step 4. When you get to the end of stitching on one side of the line, don't cut your thread. Simply raise the needle and move the fabric so the needle can enter on the opposite side of the diagonal line. This particular stitching order was designed so that you won't have any little bits of thread to remove from triangle corners once you cut your triangle squares apart.

Tip

Stitch in the same direction on both sides of the diagonal lines to avoid twisting or shirring the fabric.

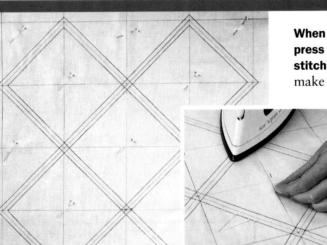

When all stitching is completed, press the fabric to "set" the stitching into the fabric. This will make cutting more accurate and the triangles will lie flatter when they are pressed open into squares.

Tip

For more even stitching, use a straight-stitch throat plate instead of a wider zigzag plate.

With a rotary cutter and ruler, cut the grid on the horizontal and vertical lines to form squares. Cut the squares diagonally along the center line to form the triangle squares.

 See Steps 3 and 4 on page 60 for directions on pressing triangle squares and trimming away dog ears.

GRID-METHOD TRIANGLE SQUARES

Bias-Square
Triangles

Your repertoire of triangle-square techniques is not complete without sampling the two basic bias-strip methods. Both are great when you need lots of triangle squares in a variety of fabrics, triangle squares in several sizes, or a limited number of same-fabric triangle squares. One of the biggest benefits of using bias strips is that slightly inconsistent seams don't affect the size of your finished triangle squares because measuring and cutting are done after the strips are sewn. You can make precise squares even if you and your sewing machine are not having a good day!

Getting Ready

Our bias-square technique combines Nancy Martin's original bias-square method with Mary Hickey's bias rectangle technique. For this method, bias strips are cut the same width as the squares that will be cut from them. To make a 3-inch finished triangle square that measures $3\frac{1}{2}$ inches with seam allowances, start with $3\frac{1}{2}$-inch bias strips. To make things easy, the examples throughout this chapter will use 3-inch finished ($3\frac{1}{2}$-inch cut-size) triangle squares.

The number of squares that can be cut across a set of strips is dependent on the number of strips used; one less square can be cut than the number of strips sewn together. So, 2 strips yield 1 square; 3 strips yield 2 squares, and so on. The length of the strip divided by the cut size of the squares will determine how many squares can be cut per row of strips. For instance, a set of 5 bias strips sewn together, each 30 inches long, will result in thirty-two $3\frac{1}{2}$-inch cut-size triangle squares (4 squares across × 8 squares per strip = 32 triangle squares).

Or, try the Double-Sewn Strip method on page 71 when your project calls for just a few bias squares.

Or, try the Double-Sewn Strip method on page 71 when your project calls for just a few bias squares.

What You'll Need

Two or more fabrics with contrasting values (at least 9" wide)

Rotary cutter and mat

24" rotary cutting ruler

Bias Square ruler

Sewing machine

¼" presser foot

100% cotton sewing thread

Iron and ironing board

Spray starch or sizing

Thread snips or embroidery scissors

Step-by-Step Strip-Set Method

1

Align the 45 degree angle marking on your rotary ruler with the selvage edge of your fabric. Cut off the corner of the fabric to create the first bias edge. Slide your ruler over so that the 2½-inch marking is in line with the cut edge.

Cut a 2½-inch strip. Continue cutting as many strips as you need of that particular fabric. To save time, layer several fabrics all with *right sides up*, and cut all at once.

Tip

For a controlled scrap look, cut background strips from the same fabric and each alternating strip from a different fabric.

BIAS-SQUARE TRIANGLES

2

Stitch together two bias strips of contrasting values along their long edges with a ¼-inch seam allowance. Position the strips as in the photograph so that when opened after stitching, their bottom edges will align. Add three more strips, continuing to alternate values. Handle the strips carefully so you don't stretch the bias edges out of shape. Stitch in the same direction each time to avoid twisting the strips. **Carefully press seams toward the darker strips from the right side to avoid pressing a tuck in the fabric.**

3

True the edge of the strip set by aligning the 45 degree angle along a seam and trimming.

Then cut a 2½-inch strip across the strip set, again keeping the 45 degree angle line on the seam. Continue to cut 2½-inch strips, periodically checking to make sure you are still cutting on the true bias.

4

Lay the 45 degree line of the Bias Square ruler on the seam, with the straight edge of the ruler flush with the fabric strip. Make your first cut, which will remove a triangle. You can sew the leftover end triangles together to make additional triangle squares, or save them for other projects.

Turn the ruler around so the 45 degree marking is now aligned with the next seam, and cut. Slide the ruler over so the 45 degree line is aligned with the next seam. Trim away the narrow strip of fabric

extending beyond the ruler and discard. Continue aligning the diagonal line with the seams and cutting squares until you have enough for your project.

Step-by-Step Double-Sewn Strip Method

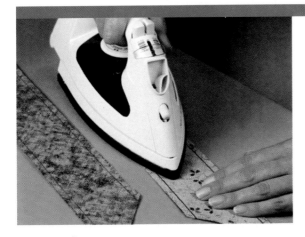

Double-sewn bias strips are cut with two layers of fabric placed *right sides together*. Cut 3½-inch-wide strips (which will yield 3-inch finished triangle squares), as shown in Step 1 of "Step-by-Step Strip-Set Method" on page 69. Then sew a pair of strips together with a ¼-inch seam allowance along *both* long edges. **Press the strip to set the stitches.**

45° line

Align the 45 degree line on your rotary ruler with the stitching line to cut right triangles, alternating sides along the strip. The resulting triangle squares will be a bit oversized. Simply trim them to 3½-inch squares with your ruler. **If you prefer, you can make a plastic template for a triangle with sides that are ½ inch longer than the desired finished size triangle squares. Use it to mark cutting lines that can then be cut with a rotary cutter or scissors.**

Remove any stitches at the tips and press open the triangles. The dog ears are usually removed in the process of cutting the alternating triangles. If not, trim them now.

Tip

Cut strips slightly wider and you won't have to remove stitches at the tips of double-sewn triangles.

Quarter-Square
Triangles

Quarter-square triangles may look and even sound complicated, but they're really just triangle squares taken one step further. The name may be a little confusing—all it means is a square made of four triangles. Instead of sewing individual triangles together (feasible, but not very fun and not very accurate), you start with a pair of triangle squares. Slice them apart, resew in different combinations, and you have some nifty patchwork to add a colorful burst of creativity to your quilts.

Getting Ready

Think of triangle squares as parents and quarter-square units as their offspring. When you cut a triangle square from corner to corner across the diagonal seam, it produces two *mirror-image* halves of a quarter-square triangle. If you sew them back together, you're right back where you started. To get the color and fabric diversity that makes a quarter-square triangle, cut a second triangle square in half diagonally. Mixing and matching these four segments into pairs of *identical* units lets you make two quarter-square triangles.

You can use any method to make parent triangle squares. However, you'll need to cut *bigger* strips, squares, or grids to account for the extra seam allowances in quarter-square triangles. For the bias-strip method, cut triangle squares ⅞ inch larger than the desired finished-size quarter-square triangle. For all other methods, add 1¼ inches to the finished size of the quarter-square triangle to calculate the size for the grid, squares, or strip width used to make the parent triangle squares.

Step-by-Step Quarter-Square Triangles

1

Cut two triangle squares along the unsewn diagonal to produce two sets of mirror-image pieced triangles. They'll have straight of grain along the short sides. If you were to sew these two mirror images together, you'd simply have the same triangle square you started with. To produce a quarter-square triangle with the like fabrics opposite one another, pair *like* images with each other. You obtain those by cutting apart *two* parent triangle squares and mixing their components.

Triangle square pairs can be sewn and cut apart to produce quarter-square triangle units without ever handling individual triangles. **Draw a line from corner to corner on the reverse side of a triangle square, along the diagonal that does not have a seam.** If your sewing machine doesn't have an accurate ¼-inch presser foot, draw two more lines, each one ¼ inch away from the first.

 See page 61 for complete details on drawing lines on fabric squares.

Align the triangle square with another triangle square, right sides together, making sure the dark half of one is facing the light half of the other. Pin to secure, and **stitch on each of the lines that are ¼ inch from the center diagonal, or use your presser foot to sew ¼ inch away from each side of the diagonal line.** Start sewing on the light triangle. That way, the presser foot will assist in keeping the butted seam allowances together.

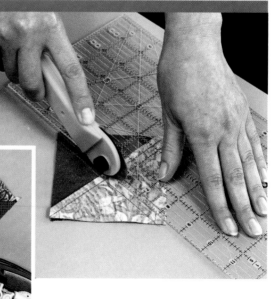

Cut the unit apart along the center line using scissors or a rotary cutter. You now have two identical quarter-square triangle units. **Press to set the stitches, then press open.** Trim away the dog ears at the ends of the diagonal seam.

P E R F E C T   P I E C I N G

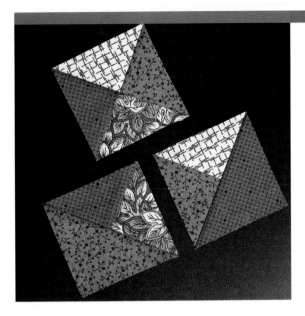

Don't limit yourself to quarter-square triangles with matching fabrics on each side. **For a scrappier look, just pair and sew together unlike parent triangle squares.** There's no limit to the creative ways you can mix and match quarter-square triangles to enhance the design of your quilt.

Another design option is to pair half of a quarter-square triangle with a single right triangle. To do that, follow Steps 1 through 4, but replace one of the triangle squares with a fabric square of identical size. Remember that the resulting units will be mirror images of each other.

You can use a layered-square method to construct *identical* quarter-square triangle halves instead of *mirror image* quarter-square triangle halves. You'll need a dark and a light square for this method, which will yield four pairs of sewn triangles—enough to make two quarter-square triangles.

Determine the square size by adding 1¼ inches to the desired finished size of the quarter-square triangle. **Draw a line from corner to corner along both diagonals on the wrong side of the lightest fabric square.**

Referring to the photo, select which type of triangle half you need and, with light and dark squares right sides together, sew ¼ inch away from marked lines, using your presser foot as a guide. If your presser foot isn't ¼ inch wide, mark the sewing lines with a pencil and ruler.

If you want the light triangles to be on the right when opened up, stitch on the right side of each drawn line. Or, if you want light triangles on the left, stitch on the left. When all four lines are stitched, cut the square apart from corner to corner along both diagonal lines.

Setting in Seams
with Ease

Perhaps no other piecing technique intimidates as many quilters as set-in seams. Yet anyone who can sew an accurate ¼-inch seam can master setting-in. Honest! All you need is a knack for using matching points and backstitching. But don't worry— we'll show you how and when to use them. Gaining proficiency at set-in seams will open up a whole new world of patterns to make, including traditional favorites like Tumbling Blocks and Double Wedding Ring, as well as all the dramatic Eight-Pointed Star designs.

Getting Ready

A set-in seam is found where three patches converge. This seam construction is also known as a Y seam, since it looks just like the capital letter Y. Because of the angle at which the patches are joined (usually 30, 45, or 60 degrees), sewing a single straight seam from one end to the other isn't possible. You need to sew two of the patches together first, and then set the third patch into the opening.

Before you sit down to sew, mark endpoints (where seam lines intersect) on your patches. These are the *exact* spots where you'll start and stop sewing. Use a window template or a template with holes at the seam intersections for marking. Even if you rotary cut your patches, make a plastic template for each shape in the set-in seam.

See "Try This!" on page 23 for directions on making templates with holes for marking endpoints.

See "Try This!" on page 23 for directions on making templates with holes for marking endpoints.

What You'll Need

Block pattern

Cut patches

Template material

Ruler

Marking pencil or fine-point permanent marking pen

Sewing machine

100% cotton sewing thread

Thread snips or embroidery scissors

Spray starch or sizing (optional)

Step-by-Step Set-In Seams

1

Using a template that includes seam allowances and holes punched at each of the seam intersections, use a pencil or marking pen to mark a dot on the *wrong* side of each fabric piece. (Or, use a window template to mark the corners where the seam lines meet.) In our Tumbling Blocks example, all pieces are the same size and shape. For other patterns, such as the Eight-Pointed Star featured on page 80, you will need a template for each shape involved in the set-in seam, namely a diamond, square, and triangle template.

See page 52 for a way to mark matching points without using a template.

See page 52 for a way to mark matching points without using a template.

2

Hold two of the pieces right sides together and pin exactly through the endpoint markings. Turn them over to verify that pinning is accurate on the underneath piece, too. **Place patches under your machine needle and manually turn the fly wheel to insert the needle through the starting dot (remove the pin at that end first).**

3

Lower the presser foot, take two stitches, backstitch two stitches only, and proceed to sew the length of the seam. Slow down as you approach the end dot and remove the pin to make sure the needle enters through the dot and not beyond it. Again, turn the fly wheel by hand, if necessary, to adjust the stitch length so the needle enters where it should. **Backstitch two stitches, and remove the fabric from the machine.**

Tip

Spraying fabric with starch *before* cutting patches for set-in seams helps control the bias edges for smooth stitching.

4

Pin the third patch of the set-in area to one of the other patches. Pin so the new piece will be on top for stitching. Again, pin exactly at the starting and stopping points, and verify that you've pinned through the dots on the underneath fabric. Stitch the seam as before, backstitching and each end to secure the seam. **Stitch from the inside corner to the outer edges of the patches.**

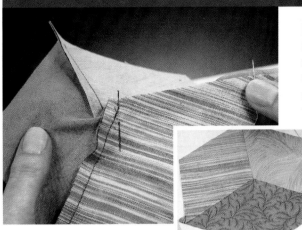

Pin along the last remaining seam line, with pins situated so you will be sewing the seam from the inner corner to the outer edge. Stitch the seam in the same manner as for the two previous seams. When you remove the patches from the sewing machine, check to see that you have not backstitched into any of the seam allowances or caught a pucker of fabric in your last seam.

Tip

When setting in the background triangles and squares in an Eight-Pointed Star, sew the bias-edged triangles in first for easier construction.

Quilters are divided about which way to press set-in seams. **No matter which way you press, one seam will overlap another, adding a bit of bulk to the finished project.** On Eight-Pointed Stars and other stars that are constructed in the same manner, consider pressing the set-in square or triangle seam toward the star. The loft of the seam will raise the design of the star, emphasizing it and making it easier to outline quilt or quilt in the ditch. For Tumbling Blocks, the patches are all the same size and shape, so pressing direction isn't as crucial.

Tip

Set-in seams often lie flat only when pressed in one direction. If that's toward the lighter fabric, trim the darker fabric to prevent show-through.

An alternate method involves pivoting at the Y rather than stopping, backstitching, and starting again. Sew two of the patches together (see Step 3), then pin the set-in patch to one of the two joined patches (see Step 4). **Manipulate the fabric to align and pin the two remaining edges together.**

Tip

Don't forget to leave your needle in the fabric when you pivot!

Start at the outer edge instead of the center. Stitch with the set-in patch on top and the already joined patches on the bottom. When you reach the end dot, don't backstitch. **Pivot the fabrics and reposition those on the bottom so they don't get caught in the next part of the seam.** Continue stitching.

SETTING IN SEAMS WITH EASE

Mastering
Eight-Seam Joins

S tars are the aristocrats of quilt blocks, which makes Eight-Pointed Stars the
    royalty. These dynamic patterns radiate from the center with energy to spare. If
    you've been caught in their spell but have hesitated to attempt one because of the
eight-seam join at the center, don't wait any longer to reach for the stars. You can use the
techniques in this lesson for eight-pointed stars and for any other multiple-seam join
when you want precisely matched points, a flat center, and a perfectly square block.

Getting Ready

Whether you rotary cut your pieces or use templates and scissors, you need to decide whether to align the straight-of-grain from point to point or along two sides of your diamond. If your fabric is striped or has a one-way design, that may be the determining factor. If it doesn't, consider cutting with the grain extending between the points of the diamond to give all sides of the diamonds the same bias angle—22½ degrees. Here's why: Instead of having two edges cut on the straight grain and two cut on 45 degree bias, the seams will have a consistent edge, which will help keep the block flat. Plus, 22½ degree bias edges stretch less than the 45 degree bias edges.

What You'll Need

Fabric for star and background

Rotary-cutting supplies, *or* **template plastic, marking pencil or fine-point permanent marking pen, and awl or ¹⁄₁₆" hole punch**

Craft and fabric scissors

Sewing machine

¼" presser foot

100% cotton sewing thread to match star fabric

Silk pins

Step-by-Step Eight-Seam Joins

1

It's easiest to piece an Eight-Pointed Star if all matching points are marked. If you are cutting with templates, pierce the templates with an awl or a ¹⁄₁₆-inch hole punch where the seam lines intersect at the narrow points of the diamonds. **Use a sharp pencil or a fine-point permanent marker to mark the points.**

Tip

When a seam ripper becomes too dull to cut threads, save it for poking matching-point holes in templates.

2

When using template-free cutting, you can mark the matching points by **laying the ¼-inch line of the ruler at the edge of the patch on either side of each point and marking an x at the seam line with a sharp pencil or a fine-point permanent marker.** Or, you can make a template as described in Step 1, and use it solely for marking the matching points. If you have a lot of points to mark, the template method could save you time since you won't have to measure each end of each diamond.

3

To reduce the bulk caused by the tips of eight diamonds meeting at the center, **trim the narrow tips of each diamond to a scant ¼ inch from the seam line.** Another way to trim the tips to reduce bulk is to use a trimming template.

 *See Step 6 on page 49 for details on creating and using a trimming template.*

4

Stitch two diamonds together along matching sides, starting and stopping with a backstitch exactly at each matching point. Do not stitch into any seam or you'll form a pleat and the block will not lie flat when it is complete. Repeat, sewing three more pairs of diamonds.

Stitch the two-diamond sets together to form two half stars. Start and stop at the matching points and backstitch, as before.

Tip

Start backstitching with the needle positioned one stitch inside the match point to avoid bulk and/or puckers at the point.

To make a perfect center match, sew only one-half of the seam at a time. Hold the two star halves right sides together, and **pin two of the facing diamonds together *exactly* at the matching points—both at the center and end of the seam.**

Starting at the center, backstitch, then stitch to the outer edge and end with a backstitch. Pin and sew the other half together, again starting from the center and stitching outward.

 Set in the corner squares and side triangles as shown in "Setting In Seams with Ease" on page 76.

Tip

An open-toe (embroidery) presser foot makes it easy to see the matching points as you stitch. Generic models are available.

MASTERING EIGHT-SEAM JOINS

Tip

If you plan to quilt in the ditch around the star, you may want to press squares and triangles over the diamonds for easier quilting.

8

Press all the seams of the diamonds in the same direction, rotating around the center. Press the diamond seams flat over the set-in patches.

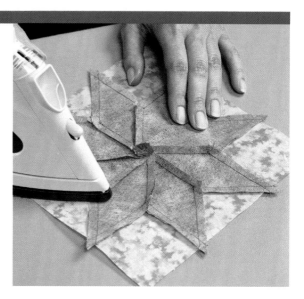

9

Press the fanned center of the star flat. A dab of water at the center of the fan will help the fabric lie flatter. Turn the block over and press from the right side.

10

Here's the result of careful cutting, piecing, and pressing: **a square, flat block with the seams radiating from a single point!**

The Quilter's
Problem Solver

Less-than-Perfect Centers

Problem	Solution
Pucker in the middle of the star.	Both problems are caused by not starting and stopping stitching exactly on the matching points. If you sew into the seam allowance a pucker or pleat is formed. Starting more than ¼ inch away from the edge of the fabric will leave a gap or hole at the center of the block. Pin carefully to be sure the points match precisely. If all else fails, correct the problem by hand stitching across the center from point to point, pulling the thread tightly as you sew.
Tiny hole in the middle of the star.	

Skill Builder

Use pin-matching for a perfect center.

There are, of course, other blocks with eight points meeting in the center. Some have all seams stitched down, such as a Pinwheel block that's made of four triangle squares. With these blocks, you can't fan the center points where they join, but you can join the centers accurately with careful pinning.

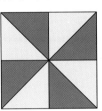

Stab a pin through the seam intersections, and open the seam to check that the match is precise. Pin on either side of the seam.

As stitching approaches the center, raise the stabbed pin so it's perpendicular to prevent the underneath half from rolling out of position. (Don't push the pin into the feed dogs.) Slowly stitch across the seam, removing the pin as it reaches the needle.

Try This!

An **alternative piecing technique** treats the set-in patches as part of the diamonds. This method reduces stress at the center and set-ins because the wider angles are easier to pin and sew.

1. Lay out patches as they'll appear in the finished block. Sew the square corners and triangles to the same side of the appropriate diamonds, back-stitching at the start and end of each seam and leaving the seam allowances free.

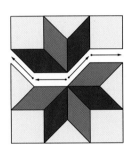

Start at center and stitch in direction of arrows

2. Stitch two diamond units together, starting at the middle of the diamond and stitching out to each end, backstitching and keeping the seam allowances free as before. Add a third diamond unit to the first two.

3. Sew the remaining five diamonds together in sequence, so one section of the star has three diamonds and one has five. Sew these two sections together, stitching from the center of the block in two steps to complete one side of the block. Repeat from the center in the other direction, completing the block.

Easy Piecing with
Partial Seams

Some quilt patterns that appear to whirl about a center shape, such as the Quartered Star, Bright Hopes, and Double Star (shown clockwise above, beginning in the upper left) look so tricky that you'd swear set-in seams were involved. But once you learn the trick of partial seams—where you sew only part of one seam so you can complete the "set-in" portion before finishing the rest of the seam— you'll be amazed at the complex blocks you can sew in a snap.

Getting Ready

Partial seams are used to assemble blocks with patches that radiate from a center shape such as a square, hexagon, or octagon. Although these blocks look as if they have set-in seams, you can avoid all the detail work setting-in requires simply by starting with a half-sewn seam.

If your pattern calls for set-in seams, study the block construction to determine if a partial seam would create a straight line for joining the next patches, letting you avoid set-in seams. (To see how to analyze a block, see the photos with Step 1, below.)

The block patterns shown in the photo to the left are perfect candidates for partial seaming. In addition to these blocks, you'll discover a wide variety of patterns in which partial seaming works, including the very simple Bright Hopes, the popular Shooting Star, and even the more complicated Feathered Star.

Step-by-Step Partial Seams

1

At first glance, some easy-to-make blocks appear to have a series of complicated set-in seams. Upon closer inspection, you'll see that by sewing a partial seam to get started, you can avoid setting in any seams. Notice the patches for the Quarter Star pattern can be laid out in two ways. **The first option looks as if two set-in seams are required. But in the other, you'll see we've arranged our patches for sewing in a different order so the first seam can be partially sewn, eliminating the need for any setting-in.**

Examine your pattern and highlight the area to be partially seamed to avoid confusion when you start to sew.

2

Join any pieces that need to be sewn together before being attached to the center patch. These pieces should be connected with complete seams. **Place the sewn patches back into your block layout.**

3

Only the first patch attached to the center piece will have a partial seam. After it is attached, you'll be able to work in either a clockwise or counterclockwise direction around the center patch (depending on your block construction), adding each new piece to the center patch with a complete seam.

To control the accuracy of your piecing, **mark the starting/stopping point on both the first patch and the center piece you'll be attaching it to.** This point should be at about the midpoint of the center patch. **Then pin the first patch onto the center, aligning the ends and matching the marked starting/stopping point.**

4

Begin stitching at the end of the pinned patches, and sew just to the midway point. Backstitch at your marked point. Athough you can begin sewing at the middle of the seam line, completing the final seam will be easier and smoother if you start at the edge and sew to the center when sewing this first part of this seam.

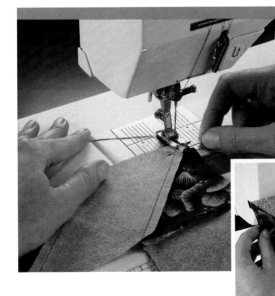

Press or finger press the partial seam. **Add the next patch, pinning it across the sewn end of the partial seam.** Stitch the seam from end to end.

Pin the partially sewn patch out of the way so it doesn't get caught as you sew subsequent seams.

Continue adding patches or units until all are attached to the center and you have come back around to the first patch. Adding the last patch will create a final straight line for the unsewn part of the first patch. **Pin the loose patch end in place, aligning the raw edges.**

Tip

Press each seam as it is sewn, since it will be crossed immediately by another line of stitching.

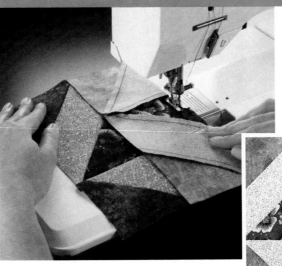

Begin stitching in the exact same spot where you ended the first partial seam. Backstitch, keeping the stitching line smooth. Stitch to the end of the seam and press.

Tip

Take care not to stretch or distort the half-stitched patch during the process of sewing the other seams.

E A S Y   P I E C I N G   W I T H   P A R T I A L   S E A M S

Incredibly Easy
Curved Seams

Curved shapes give a whole new dimension to quilt designs, adding interest and counterpoint to the straight lines and angles seen in most patchwork quilts. At their simplest, curved pieces can be sewn into square blocks and assembled in rows, as in Drunkard's Path. Or a quilt can contain nothing but curves, as in the perennial favorite, Double Wedding Ring. Curves do take a little extra time to prepare, pin, and sew, but once you've mastered a few basic tricks, curved piecing becomes easy.

Getting Ready

If you've never sewn curves before, you'll find that shallow arcs are easier to sew than deep ones. You may want to start out with a pattern like Robbing Peter to Pay Paul, which has gently curved shapes. The methods given in this lesson will help you sew any type of curve with ease.

Templates are a necessity, whether you buy ready-made acrylic templates or make your own. When making templates, be sure to copy the matching points from the printed pattern so you can transfer the marks to your fabric pieces for accurate matching and pinning.

Directional-print fabrics may dictate how you position templates on the fabric, but for easiest piecing, place templates so any straight edges are on the straight grain and the deepest part of the curves are on the bias.

Some curved patchwork, like the Double Wedding Ring, also involves set-in piecing, so you may also want to read "Setting In Seams with Ease" on page 76.

What You'll Need

Block pattern

Assorted fabrics

Template material and marking pen or pencil *or* ready-made templates

Fabric and craft scissors

Silk pins

Sewing machine

100% cotton sewing thread

Stiletto or long pin

Step-by-Step Curved Seams

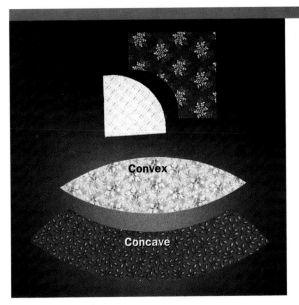

1

To create a simple curved line in fabric involves joining a *concave* to a *convex* curve. **The concave curve bends inward.** In the Drunkard's Path block, the piece that is roughly shaped like an L has a concave curve. In the Double Wedding Ring, wedding band arcs and the center portion of the block both have concave curves. **The convex curve rounds outward,** like the Drunkard's Path wedge-of-pie piece or the melon wedge of the Double Wedding Ring.

2

Trace templates on the wrong sides of the fabrics. When using hand piecing templates, add seam allowances as you cut the fabric. Machine piecing templates should already include seam allowances. **But be sure to mark end points and other matching points from the pattern on your fabric.**

To mark the midpoint, fold each patch in half and crease with your fingernail. You can mark the quarter-points for matching by folding in half again and creasing. Curved edges are cut on the bias, so take care not to stretch them as you fold and crease.

Tip

Sew scant ¼" seam allowances to make easing the fullness easier.

3

When seam allowances are added to curved shapes, the two curves become different sizes, so the fabric has to be *eased* to fit. That's when the excess fabric of the convex curve is gently (and slowly) maneuvered to fit the smaller concave curve.

Place the two patches right sides together, with the *concave* piece on top facing you. This will make it easier for you to manipulate the fabric as you pin the two opposite shaped curves together. **Pin at the midpoints. Turn the patches over to make sure they're pinned accurately.**

4

With the midpoints already pinned together, match and pin the ends of the patches. The cut edges should be aligned at the sides. (Note: For Double Wedding Ring or other patterns that involve set-in piecing, match the *end points* for sewing, rather than the cut ends of the fabric.)

Pin through the quarter-points and any marked matching points. Some quilters pin all along the seam line. Others pin only the first half of the seam, stopping at the center to rearrange and pin for the second half. Try both methods to see which works best for you.

Tip

Pin through only a few threads of the fabrics, so pins are easy to maneuver in the easing process.

Very sharp curves usually require clipping in order for the two pieces to fit together. **Clip the deepest part of the arc to a depth of ⅛ inch at close intervals.** Don't clip right to the seam line or you may create small indentations on the right side of the finished seam. Deep clips also severely weaken the seam.

6

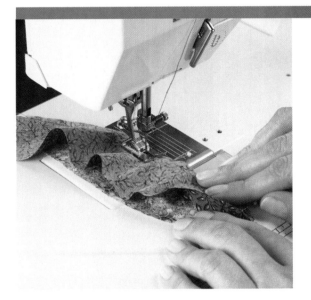

Gentle curves don't need to be clipped. **The bias edges of the curve will give enough flexibility to spread the concave curve around to fit the convex piece.** Use your fingertips, a stiletto, or a long pin to adjust the fabric as you sew.

7

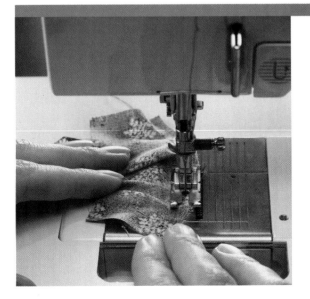

Notice that when you pin, the curved pieces begin to arch and not lie flat. That's just how they'll behave when you start to sew. Begin at one end and stitch slowly and carefully.

Also note that because the sewing machine stitches in a straight line, **you must stop and pivot slightly in order to retain the arc of the curve.** Remove the pins as you come to them.

Tip

An automatic needle-down feature makes easy work of stopping and pivoting.

INCREDIBLY EASY CURVED SEAMS

8

It's essential to keep the cut edges of both pieces aligned or you'll end up with a lumpy seam line rather than a smooth curve. Even if you have pinned heavily, check and adjust the two pieces as you sew the seam lines together. **Hold the underneath fabric steady with your left hand while you use a pin or stiletto to gently adjust the top fabric as they pass under the presser foot.** Continue pivoting and adjusting all the way along the curve.

By stitching slowly and readjusting the fabric as needed, you can avoid forming the dreaded pleat on the piece underneath.

9

Tip

To remove any stubborn puckers around the curve, mist with a spray water bottle and press again.

With a shallow curve, the seam allowance can usually be pressed to either side, depending on where the dark fabric is and on your quilting plan. (See "Pressing for Precision" on page 40.) With a deeper curve, the seam allowance will fall more easily into the convex piece, although some fabrics will have a mind of their own. **Press lightly from the wrong side of the fabric to set the direction of the seam allowance.** Do final pressing from the right side to ensure that the curve is smooth and flat, without any pleats.

10

The curved patches are ready to be joined in rows to complete the block or quilt rows.

The Quilter's
Problem Solver

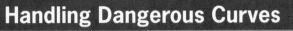

Handling Dangerous Curves

Problem	Solution
After sewing the curves, block or unit is distorted.	Original pinning may have been slightly off-center. Or stitching may have wandered off the line in some areas. If the distortion is not great, make a template for the shape of the unit and "true up" the patch to make it square. If that means you'll be cutting off a point or altering the pattern, it's best to remake the unit.
Fabric won't cooperate as it should to make curves match up.	With some fabrics, the stretching and pushing action for curved piecing may work more easily with the concave piece on top. It is a matter of personal preference as to which way you place and stitch the pieces. If you sew with the convex piece on top, take care not to stitch pleats into either piece at the seam line.
Seam is bulky due to extra fabric in the curve.	The deeper the curve, the more "extra" fabric you'll have in the seam allowance. If small pleats are formed in the seam allowance due to pressing, not stitching, you can trim away some of their bulk with the tip of your embroidery scissors. Don't cut too close to the stitching line. Re-press for a smooth look.

Skill Builder

These three secrets will let you stitch curves like a pro.

❏ Pivot often to maneuver the straight-stitching machine around the curved seam line. Pivot every few stitches for a flowing curve.

❏ Avoid clipping seam allowances (except for very deep curves), since clips can promote little dimples and peaks in the finished curve as well as allow the edge to stretch.

❏ Curves are cut on the bias, so the fabric is very flexible and easy to manipulate. But don't overwork the fabric, or it will stretch out of shape.

Try This!

In her book *Freedom in Design*, Mia Rozmyn uses finished-size **freezer paper templates** for curved piecing. After pressing the freezer paper to the fabric, she cuts the fabric ¼ inch away from the paper for seam allowances. Then she sews a line of stay stitching (6 stitches per inch) at the edge of the freezer paper, just inside the seam allowance. The freezer paper is removed and the curved pieces joined, using registration marks, creases, and pinning just as with traditional curved piecing. The stay stitching stabilizes the bias edges of the curves and the pieces fit together easily and smoothly. The stay stitches also act as a stitching guide for piecing.

Staystitching

Freezer paper template

Wrong side of fabric

The Basics of
Paper Foundation Piecing

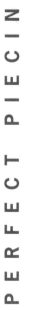

W ith this simple technique, your piecing skills will take a quantum leap. Sewing
the fabric patches for a block onto a paper foundation makes the whole piecing
process faster, easier, and unbelievably accurate. You can become an instant
pro at matching narrow points, taming bias edges, and managing tiny pieces.

Getting Ready

Estimating the yardage for paper foundation piecing is not an exact science. More fabric is needed than for template-cut patches because extra is trimmed away after the patches are sewn. You may need up to twice as much fabric if numerous patches are small and you are not particularly conservative about positioning strips for sewing. Plan on a generous amount of fabric for a paper foundation pieced project. Scrap quilts are ideal for this method because a set amount of a particular fabric is not essential.

Number the sections within the block to establish the piecing order. Blocks specially designed for paper piecing will have this numbered order of assembly indicated.

What You'll Need

Block pattern traced or photocopied onto paper foundation

Refer to "Easy and Accurate Foundation Preparation" on page 102 for seven ways to make foundations.

Fabrics for block

Sewing machine

Iron and ironing board

Fabric scissors

Silk pins

Rotary-cutting supplies (optional)

Step-by-Step Foundation Piecing

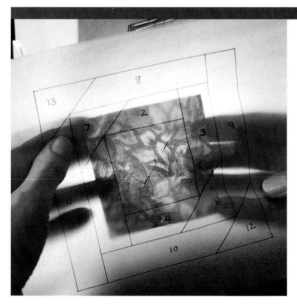

1

Here's a basic rule to remember: **Sew on the marked side of the paper, and place the fabric on the plain side of the paper.** As you position fabric pieces and sew, you will be flipping back and forth between both sides.

2

Cut the fabric for Patch 1 about 1 inch larger all around than the area it will be covering. **Center the fabric under Patch 1, with the wrong side of the fabric facing the plain side of the paper.** If it is difficult to see through the paper, hold the patch in place and then hold the layers up to the light. When the fabric is centered, pin in place from the marked side.

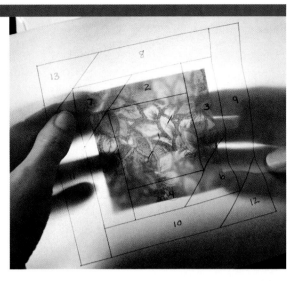

3

Cut the fabric for Patch 2 large enough to extend beyond the sewing lines on all sides. **Lay the right side of Fabric Patch 2 against the right side of Fabric Patch 1.** Make sure the raw edge of Fabric Patch 2 extends at least ¼ inch beyond the sewing line.

Use a "shadowing" technique to check placement of the second fabric patch. **With the marked side of the paper facing you, hold the foundation up to the light and look for the shadow of the second patch.** In addition to your sewing machine light, a sunny window or a small reading light will also work.

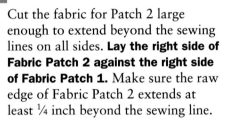

4

Turn to the marked side of the foundation. Set the stitch length for 14 to 18 stitches per inch. **Begin and end 2 or 3 stitches beyond the line and stitch through the paper and the two layers of fabric. Follow the drawn line precisely.**

5

Clip threads close to the stitching. **Then, trim the seam allowance to a scant ¼ inch using either sewing scissors or a rotary cutter.** Fold under the paper foundation so fabric in the seam allowance extends out and away from the paper. Eyeball the ¼ inch as you trim with your scissors, or lay fabric on a cutting mat and measure ¼ inch with a ruler, then trim away excess with your rotary cutter. (See Step 7 for an example of trimming with a rotary cutter.)

6

Flip open Fabric Patch 2 and press the seam. You may finger press or use an iron. Make sure Fabric Patch 2 is flat before pinning on the marked side to hold it in place while Fabric Patch 3 is being added.

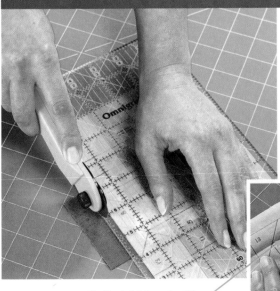

7

This step is entirely optional, but you may find it handy. **Trim the seam allowance to ¼ inch where the fabric overlaps the next sewing line.** Trimming the excess like this after each line of stitching provides an accurate placement guide when you are adding subsequent patches. **To make trimming easy, fold under the paper foundation so fabric extends out and away from the paper.** Lay the fabric on a cutting mat and measure ¼ inch with a ruler, then trim away the excess with your rotary cutter.

Optional trimming line

Continue adding fabric patches in numerical order, as described in Steps 3 through 6, until each patch on the foundation is covered. **Make sure the patches extend beyond the outside edges of the block by at least ¼ inch.**

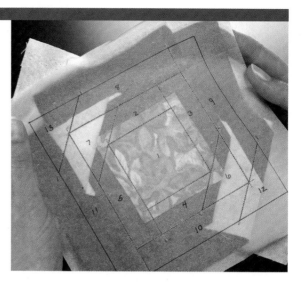

A rotary cutter and ruler make this step easy and accurate.

Turn the block paper side up and trim ¼ inch away from the outer seam line. If your paper foundation pattern has this cutting line indicated, use it as a guide for trimming. One important exception: If you've photocopied your foundation pattern, some distortion may have crept in and the marked seam allowance may not be a perfect ¼ inch. The safest thing then is to measure ¼ inch from the outer seam line, and trim. Do this by placing the ¼-inch guide on your ruler on top of the seam line, then cut. Use this same approach if your pattern does not have a cutting line indicated.

Leave the foundation paper in place until the block is joined with other blocks or sashing to complete the quilt top, then remove. The paper backing provides extra stability as you assemble the quilt. Be sure to double-check that the fabric edges of the blocks are flat and not folded back (hidden behind the foundations) when you sew the seams.

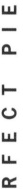

The Quilter's Problem Solver

Removing Paper Foundations

Problem	Solution
Stitches loosen when paper is torn away.	This is the tell-tale sign that you need to use smaller stitches. A good rule is the thicker the paper, the smaller the stitches. For typing or photocopier paper, use 22 stitches per inch. For thin paper, like tracing or tear-away paper, use 14 to 18 stitches per inch.
Paper is hard to tear away.	Freezer paper is notoriously hard to remove. Smaller stitches help perforate the paper and make it easier to remove, so try a smaller stitch length than you've been using. With any paper, fold along the stitched line first, then rip along the stitches (the way you fold and then tear stamps from a perforated sheet).
Little pieces of paper are tricky to remove.	Use the point of a seam ripper, a pair of tweezers, or the blunt end of a large tapestry needle to help get out those pesky little bits.

Skill Builder

Use these tips when pressing fabric on a paper foundation.

❑ Place a paper towel between the block and your iron to protect the paper.

❑ Use low steam.

❑ Press from the fabric side. If you press on the other side, the paper will absorb too much steam and start to curl.

❑ When you sew blocks together, press each seam open and flat as you go.

Try This!

Finger pressing can be taken quite literally—just run your pointer finger or thumb firmly along the right side of the seam line to make the joined patches lie flat. However, if you're doing a lot of paper foundation piecing at one sitting, your finger may end up getting sore. If that's the case, try pressing with a wooden Popsicle stick. Or close the blades of your sewing shears and run the outside edges of the blades along the seam line to press open.

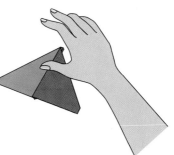

Easy and Accurate
Foundation Preparation

It's easy to understand why foundation piecing is taking the quilt world by storm. With a base on which to piece, quilters of all skill levels can achieve amazing precision and stability with any type of fabric. Once you know more about the advantages and disadvantages of different foundation materials and how to make your own foundations, you'll be able to plan and piece original designs and innovative color sequences.

Getting Ready

Study blocks to learn to "read" the best piecing order. You'll be amazed at how many blocks can be foundation pieced in one way or another. The goal is to piece in the easiest and most efficient order.

Blocks that are pieced around the center, from the side, or diagonally across the block without being interrupted by set-in pieces or abutting seams can be pieced on a single foundation.

If there are abutting seams, look for another option. Can you divide the block into foundation segments? A Schoolhouse block is one example, where the house, roof, and chimney areas each become a separate foundation segment. Some blocks divide neatly in halves, quarters, eighths, or rows for segment piecing; others require asymmetrical division.

Finally, you can combine foundation piecing with conventional piecing by using the foundation to control difficult portions of blocks such as New York Beauty or Pickle Dish.

Fabric or nonwoven interfacing

Tracing, freezer, typing, or newsprint paper, *or* removable interfacing

Mechanical pencil or marking pen

Iron and ironing board

Heat transfer pencil and typing paper or baking parchment

Sewing machine

Photocopy machine

Tracing wheel and dressmaker's carbon

Stencil

Fabric and craft scissors

Spray starch or sizing (optional)

Computer (optional)

Step-by-Step Foundation Preparation

Selecting Foundation Material

There are many choices for foundations, and each is useful for specific types of projects. Permanent foundations are left in place, making great stabilizers for clothing or decorator items. Lightweight fabric or nonwoven interfacings can be used as permanent foundations.

Temporary foundations are best for hand quilting, since there's no extra layer to quilt through. Lightweight, nonwoven interfacings as well as many types of paper are suitable. Generally, lighter-weight foundations such as tissue paper or parchment are easiest to remove.

Tip

Prewash fabric foundations. Then, iron them with spray starch or sizing for easier drawing.

FOUNDATION PREPARATION

103

Tracing Patterns

Any foundation material can be marked with a pencil. A mechanical pencil is a good choice because it stays sharp, which aids in accuracy. Tape or pin the foundation to the pattern so it will not shift out of position during tracing. **Position the ruler slightly back from the line being traced so the pencil will draw exactly on the line.** Always check to be sure you have traced all the lines before lifting the paper from the pattern.

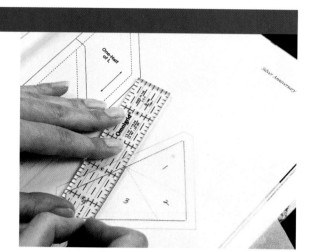

Heat Transfer

Tip

Sharpen the pencil between each tracing. The lead is soft and the point will wear away easily.

Heat transfer is an efficient method for making multiple, identical foundations on fabric or interfacing. **Trace a pattern with a transfer pencil onto typing paper with a high rag content or baking parchment—both can withstand the heat of an iron. After tracing, position the paper with the drawn side against fabric. Hold a hot, dry iron on the paper until the design under the iron is transferred to the fabric.** If the design is larger than the iron, repeat until the entire pattern is transferred. Several transfers can be made before you will need to retrace the lines on the same paper.

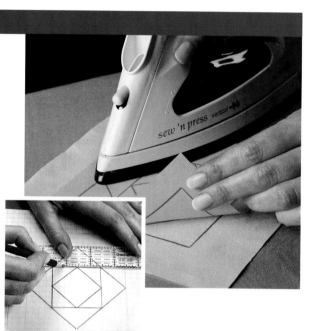

Needle Punching

Tip

Before removing the pattern, turn the stack over to be sure all lines are punched. It's easy to miss one!

Needle punching is a quick and easy method for making up to 12 identical paper foundations in one step. And because they're prepunched, they're also easy to remove from the finished block. **Pin a traced pattern to a stack of tracing paper. Use an unthreaded sewing machine to "sew" along each line of the pattern.** The traced pattern can be reused two or three times before it starts to tear from the stitching.

The underneath side of each foundation will be rough from the motion of the needle, which helps hold the fabric patches in place for piecing.

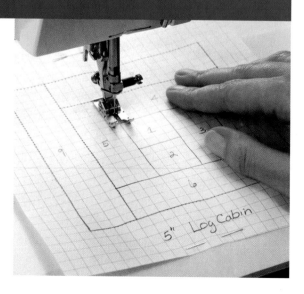

Photocopying

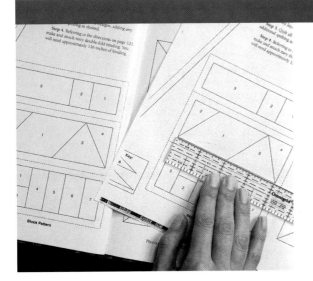

Photocopying a pattern seems an easy way to produce foundations, but use this method with discretion. **All copy machines distort in at least one direction.** On a small block, this can be a problem that negates the advantage of unlimited copies. Plus, copy machine paper is thicker than other choices and requires a very short stitch to avoid loose threads after the paper is removed. If using a copier, try substituting thinner paper. Copy only from an original to avoid compounding the distortion inherent in the machine.

Tip

Always check the marked foundation against the original pattern for accuracy, regardless of the method used.

Laser Printing

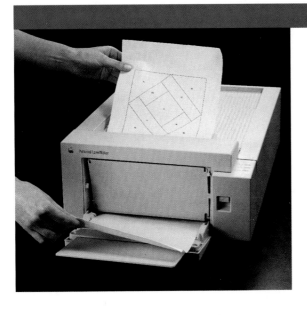

Computer printing has the advantages of photocopying—lots of identical copies are quick to make—without the disadvantages. You're limited only by the size of the printer. As long as you draft your pattern accurately on your computer (or download an accurate one from the Internet), your printed pattern will be accurate, too. **And, with many laser printers, you can make *fabric* foundations. Iron fabric onto freezer paper, trim it to fit the paper tray, and feed it through printer.** Like photocopy paper, standard computer paper will require a smaller stitch for best results.

Carbon & Tracing Wheel

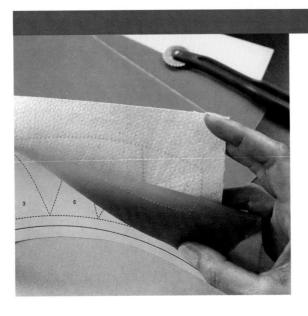

A tracing wheel can be used with dressmaker's carbon to mark fabric. Layer several pieces of fabric with a sheet of carbon paper face down between each one. **When using a tracing wheel, move the ruler slightly back from the line being copied so the tracing wheel will roll exactly on the line.** Paper foundations can also be marked this way, with or without the carbon paper. If you don't use carbon paper, you'll see just the indentations that the spiked wheel made in the papers.

FOUNDATION PREPARATION

Stencils

Tip

Before making multiple foundations, make one sample to be sure you're tracing along the correct side of every slot for an accurate pattern.

Premade stencils for marking foundations are available at most quilt shops and come in a variety of block and border designs. **When using stencils to mark a foundation, take care not to bend the plastic when tracing and to trace along the outer edge of the slot.** If you vary your drawing from one side of the opening to the other, your foundations will not all be identical. You can trace each foundation individually, or speed things up by using a heat transfer pen or pencil to trace designs. Then you can iron the pattern onto several foundations from each tracing.

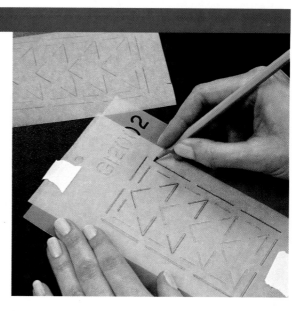

Purchased Foundations

Premarked foundations are available in a wide range of patterns and sizes. They are available both in fabric and paper. While they'll save you time because you won't have to make your own foundations, the instructions vary in the amount of detail provided from one manufacturer to another.

 See "The Basics of Paper Foundation Piecing" on page 96 if your purchased foundations contain no instructions.

Adding Seam Allowances

No matter what foundation material you use or how you mark the pattern on it, you have the option of adding the outer ¼-inch seam allowance around the foundation. **When the seam allowance is included on the foundation, the edges of the block can be machine basted to the seam allowance.** This holds the fabric taut against the foundation, so fabric won't shift at the edge of the blocks when they are being sewn together. **When basting on paper, use a long stitch so the thread can be removed easily before you tear the paper away.** There is no need to remove basting from permanent foundations.

The Quilter's
Problem Solver

The Mystery of Backward Blocks

Problem	Solution
The block is reversed from the pattern.	This happens when asymmetrical blocks are stitched with the foundation facing up and the fabric underneath. Pieced blocks are *mirror images* of the drawn pattern. Make the block look like the original pattern on transparent foundations by marking "top" on the plain or unmarked side of the foundation and piecing with fabric directly against the drawn side. (For needle-punched foundations, place fabric on smooth side of foundation and stitch on rough side.) For opaque foundations, reverse the drawing process. Retrace the master pattern on the back of the pattern, using a light table or window. Or, use carbon paper with the carbon side against the back of the pattern while you retrace the original lines. Use the carbon side of the drawing as your master pattern.
One of the segments of a multi-segment block is backward and won't fit into the block.	This is caused when one of the segments is pieced on the wrong side of the foundation. Before cutting a foundation into segments, mark them all with "top" so none will be inadvertently pieced in a mirror image.

Skill Builder

There are two easy ways to make foundations for blocks pieced in two or more segments.

❏ Trace the complete block as a unit (without seam allowances), cutting it into segments before piecing. That way there is no possibility of tracing error, since the foundations will fit together exactly as they are traced.

❏ Or, draw each segment separately so you can add a seam allowance to the individual segment foundations. The benefit? You can baste the edges of the segments to the foundations for added stability.

Try This!

It's easy to avoid errors by marking piecing order, color placement, and fabric choices directly on the foundation.

Use different colors to mark different types of notations. For instance, mark piecing order with pencil and color placement with colored markers. If you are making different colorations of the same block, mark and piece one foundation to be sure it's correct. Use it as a model to mark and piece all the blocks with that coloration before proceeding to the next variation.

When using different fabrics of the same color, make a master foundation sheet with fabric swatches to use as a reference for the fabric code on the foundations. For instance, label red fabric R-1, R-2, and R-3 beside each fabric on the master sheet. Blue would be B-1, B-2, and so on.

Creative
Crazy Piecing

Crazy piecing has fascinated quilters and quilt lovers alike for over a century, ever since lavishly embellished crazy quilts became all the rage in fashionable Victorian parlors. Today's quilters still enjoy the charm of crazy quilting, whether they replicate the Victorian style with elegant fabrics and extravagant stitchery and embellishment or use it in more contemporary ways. Because crazy piecing is random, there's no need to match points and seams, which can be delightfully liberating. You also get the fun of creating your own "fabric" as you mix bits and pieces to create a larger whole.

Getting Ready

Crazy piecing can combine hand and machine work, piecing, and appliqué. It's a great way to use scraps and bits of special fabrics. For best results, select a palette of compatible colors. Whether you buy yardage or use what you have, cut your fabrics into easy-to-use pieces, such as fat quarters or fat eighths. You don't need to limit your fabric selections to 100 percent cotton. Satins, velvets, brocades, and other fabrics will give you the true flavor of Victorian crazy piecing.

A foundation is always used because fabric placement is done without regard to grain line, and the fabrics themselves may be of differing weights and fiber content. Choose a permanent foundation, such as muslin, when the piece will be embellished and finished without quilting or when you are piecing by hand. Paper is the best choice if you'll be hand quilting, since it's removable.

- **Selection of fabrics**
- **Foundation material**
- **Fabric scissors**
- **Silk pins**
- **Ruler**
- **Sewing machine**
- **100% cotton sewing thread**
- **Iron and ironing board**
- **Rotary-cutting supplies**
- **Thread, floss, beads, and charms for embellishment (optional)**

See "Easy and Accurate Foundation Preparation" on page 103 for more information on selecting the best foundation for your project.

Step-by-Step Crazy Piecing

1

Cut your choice of foundation material to the *finished* size and shape for your project, which could be individual blocks or a larger, single foundation, such as a vest front. Then cut the shape for the first patch. This patch should have three, five, or six sides to provide a nice flow in the piecing (avoid starting with a square), and be a size that is proportional to the size of your foundation. **Lay the first patch right side up, and pin it near the center.** The first piece is the only one that should be precut to a specific shape.

CREATIVE CRAZY PIECING

2

Align an uncut piece of fabric along one edge of the first piece with right sides together. Sew through all layers, starting and stopping at each end of the first piece. You won't be able to see the first patch underneath the second fabric, so use a straight pin to mark the starting and stopping points. Stitching must be in a straight line so the fabric will lie flat when it is pressed open.

3

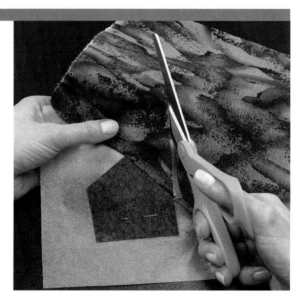

Press open the second piece and trim it to the desired shape. Trim so the sides of the cut edge are *even with* or *inside* the lines formed by edges of the previous piece. If the second fabric extends beyond the edges of the previous piece, an inside angle will be formed, which hinders piecing. Pin the second piece to the foundation to hold in position for adding the next piece.

4

Continue adding pieces, always stitching along the entire edge of the previous piece or pieces, but not beyond them. Press and pin each newly added fabric flat against the foundation so the finished size will be correct. When sewing a light fabric over a darker one, make sure the light fabric covers the raw edge of the darker one to avoid shadow-through.

To keep the piecing proportional, don't just add new pieces along one edge of the patchwork. Work on all sides for a balanced look.

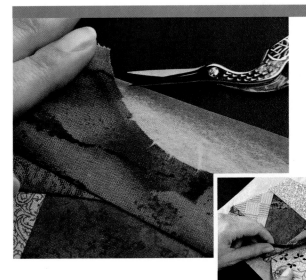

To form a curve, start with a piece of fabric that has an inside right angle. **Clip the seam allowance along the angle so it's easier to turn the seam under and position it over previous piecing.** Pin it in place and trim it to the desired size, following the guidelines for avoiding an inside angle. Leave it pinned as you continue adding pieces around its remaining (uncurved) edges. The curve will be closed with hand appliqué or embellishment after the whole foundation is completed.

You can cut an angle to form a curve in a piece already stitched to the foundation. **For a graceful curve, cut the sides of a long piece of fabric for the angle/concave curve as in Step 5.** Clip the angle.

While a convex curve could be laid on top of the angle and appliquéd, it's much easier to turn under the edges of a concave curve. **Place the next fabric to be added *under* the angle and turn under the top seam allowance to form a concave curve.** Pin the curved edge in place and continue piecing.

Tip

Use curves to visually break up a long, straight line of a single fabric.

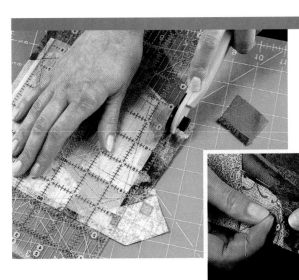

Fabric should overhang the edges of the foundation by at least ¼ inch. **When the foundation is covered, turn it to the wrong side and trim the fabric so a ¼-inch seam allowance extends beyond the foundation.**

Close the curves with a blind stitch or embellishment, such as lace, ribbon, or embroidery stitches. If you hand blind stitch, don't sew through the foundation. It will be easier to remove if you simply sew the two crazy patches together and leave the foundation free.

Tip

Turn crazy piecing into instant crazy quilting by adding a layer of batting to the foundation.

CREATIVE CRAZY PIECING

String Piecing
on Foundations

S tring piecing was born of hard times, decades ago, when scraps from household sewing and serviceable portions of worn clothing were turned into quick and inexpensive bed covers. This melding of utility and beauty retains its popularity, as quilters today use string piecing to re-create the look of antique quilts, to make new and exciting contemporary quilts, and to just plain have fun. An undemanding technique, string piecing is a great way to use leftover fabric. The only limitation is your imagination!

Getting Ready

String piecing is related to both crazy and strip piecing but has its own unique characteristics. While done on a foundation, it differs from crazy piecing because the piecing is linear rather than made from a variety of shapes. It differs from strip piecing because the widths are random, rather than preplanned. In some cases, the foundation can be the size of an entire block. Or, you can create "yardage" from which shapes are cut, then assembled to make a block. When cutting shapes from string-pieced yardage, freezer paper is a good foundation choice. It's easy to draw around a template onto freezer paper, plus it's easy to cut without distortion, especially pieces with bias edges.

Before you get started, be forewarned: String piecing is fun. But the more strips you string together, the more strings you cut. Soon they'll be multiplying and you'll never use them all!

See "Easy and Accurate Foundation Preparation" on page 102 for a discussion of foundation materials.

Step-by-Step String Piecing

1

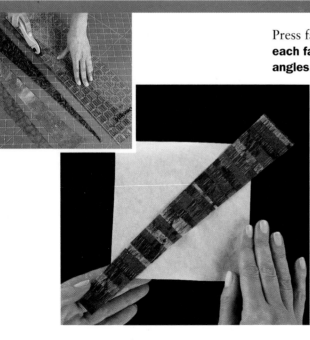

Press fabrics. **Rotary cut strips from each fabric in varying widths and angles.** If you prefer to use scissors, mark cutting lines with a pencil and ruler before cutting to ensure that edges are straight. **Pin the first strip across the foundation, with the ends extending beyond it.** The strip can be placed at any angle on the foundation.

Tip

Recycle unused strips from other strip-pieced projects, irregular shaped strips from straightening cuts, and trimmings from quilt backing leftovers.

STRING PIECING ON FOUNDATIONS

Align the next strip along one edge of the first, right sides together. Stitch through all layers ¼ inch from the fabric edges. (As with other types of foundation piecing, use a shorter stitch length for string piecing to make it easier to remove the foundation.) If the second strip is a lighter color than the first one, make the seam allowance of the lighter fabric slightly greater than ¼ inch to avoid shadow-through. Be sure the bottom fabric has an adequate seam allowance when doing this.

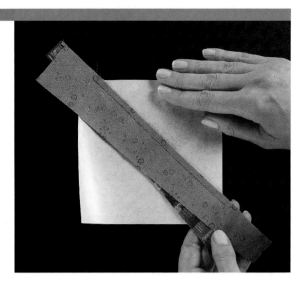

3

Set the stitches by pressing the seam before it is opened. **Then open the top strip so it's right side up and press firmly.** Take care to avoid pressing in a tuck. **Pin the strip to the foundation, keeping the pins out of the seam allowance,** to hold it taut and ready for adding the next strip. Don't trim the excess strip length. Just let the ends extend beyond the foundation for now.

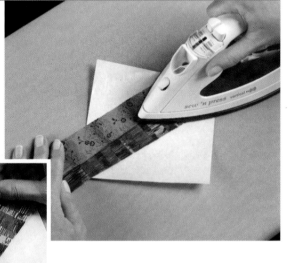

4

Place strips on both edges of the piecing and stitch them in place. This efficient way of adding strips means you can sew two strips each time before setting the stitches and pressing open. Pin the bottom fabric to the foundation, but don't pin the strips you'll be adding so the presser foot does not push the fabric into a pleat.

When the foundation is completely covered with strings, turn it to the wrong side. **Trim away the excess fabric, leaving a ¼-inch seam allowance extending beyond the foundation.** The edge of the foundation will be the seam line when the blocks are joined.

Tip

For a fun look, cut up string-pieced blocks and recombine them—either with each other or with solid fabrics.

You can string piece smaller units or patches just as you would string piece a whole quilt block. **Cut a *finished-size* foundation for each patch and string piece them individually,** using the same sequence as described above. Because foundations are cut to finished size, there is no paper in the seam allowance, so there is less bulk in the seams. Removal of the foundation is easier, too.

Tip

Possibilities for string-pieced designs are endless. Try different block shapes such as rectangles, triangles, or hexagons. Let your imagination play!

To create string-pieced yardage for cutting patchwork shapes, **trace around templates on the *wrong* side of the foundation.** Use a rotary cutter and ruler to cut out straight-edged shapes. A scissors is necessary for cutting curved pieces.

If your templates don't include seam allowances, leave room between your shapes for seam allowances. **Measure from the drawn line of the template and cut ¼-inch seam allowances on all sides of each template.** While this method is quicker than string piecing onto individual foundations, there will be foundation paper in the seam allowances, which adds bulk to seams.

Tip

Sew string-pieced blocks together with 14 to 16 stitches per inch, then press seams open to reduce bulk.

Up-to-Date
Hand Piecing

Hand piecing may seem like a low-tech way to stitch, but it's surprisingly well suited to our fast-paced lives. You can pick it up and sew on the go, stitching in spare moments at Little League games, waiting in the doctor's office, or while riding in the car (on the passenger side, of course!). Hand piecing has the reputation of being slow, but once you get the rhythm, the stitches fly along. Even dyed-in-the-wool machine piecers have to admire the high social quotient—you can hand piece while visiting with friends or in the midst of family activities.

Getting Ready

Make *finished-size* templates from sturdy material, such as template plastic, and mark the seam lines on the wrong side of the fabric. English paper piecing is a form of foundation piecing where each patch has a separate foundation. It is a precise way to piece intricately shaped designs and is often used with traditional One-Patch quilts such as Grandmother's Flower Garden, as well as for art quilts. Foundations can be purchased, or you can make your own from card stock or freezer paper.

Quilters differ on the needles they like to use for hand piecing. Some prefer quilting betweens—they're short and easy to control. Others like the length of appliqué needles— they're easy to feed fabric onto. Try both and decide for yourself.

 *See "Cutting Patches with Templates" on page 18 for instructions on making hand-piecing templates.*

What You'll Need

Cut and marked patches

Matching 100% cotton thread

Needles: size 8 or 10 appliqué (sharps) or quilting (betweens)

Silk pins

Pincushion

Thimble

Thread snips or embroidery scissors

Template plastic (for traditional piecing)

Freezer paper or card stock (for English paper piecing)

Craft scissors (for English paper piecing)

Step-by-Step Traditional Hand Piecing

1

Match the stitching lines, and pin the patches right sides together. Pin perpendicularly at the beginning and end of the seam. Pin horizontally along the seam line between the endpoint pins to keep the seam lines matched precisely.

Tip

To prevent tangling, thread the needle before cutting thread off the spool. Clip an 18" length and knot the spool end.

2

Tip

Match thread to the darkest fabric being sewn; medium-gray thread usually works well for multicolor fabric.

Leaving the seam allowance free, insert the needle at the beginning of the marked seam. You can start either with a small knot and a backstitch, or a backstitch alone. **To form a backstitch, take a small stitch at the beginning of the seam line, reinsert the needle at the place it entered at the beginning of the stitch, and come back up through the fabric at the same place as the first stitch.** Tug on the thread to check that it's secure.

3

Tip

If you are using several colors of thread, thread each into its own needle for quick color changes.

Feed from three to five stitches onto the needle at a time. Hold the needle stationary and move the fabric onto it, rather than moving the needle through the fabric. Stitches should be as small as possible. Pull the thread tight so the patches are held together firmly. For a secure seam, periodically insert a backstitch, as described in Step 2. **End a line of stitching with another backstitch and a loop knot.**

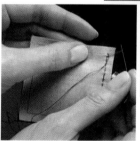

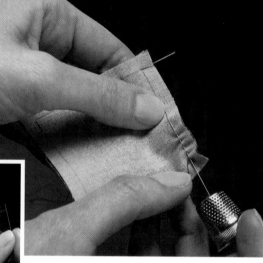

4

Tip

Pressing as you go isn't crucial since seam allowances aren't stitched down. Finger press, but don't use an iron until the block is complete.

When crossing seam intersections, keep the seam allowances free. Backstitch just before the intersection, slip the needle through both fabrics to the other side, and backstitch again. Continue piecing as before.

Step-by-Step English Paper Piecing

Foundations for English paper piecing are the *finished* size of the block, while fabric patches are cut from a template that includes the seam allowance. A window template (see Step 7 on page 21) works great, since it provides both marking lines on one template. You can also purchase ready-made papers at your quilt shop.

To make foundations, draw shapes nested together on paper. Layer two or three sheets of paper, and staple them together in the middle of each drawn shape to prevent layers from slipping during cutting. Cut shapes apart and remove the staples.

Advertising inserts in magazines are just the right weight to use for English paper piecing foundations.

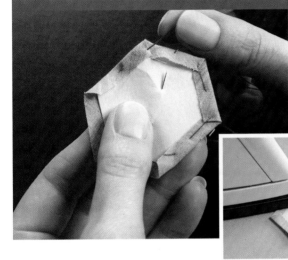

If you use a card-stock foundation, place it on the wrong side of the patch and **baste the seam allowance over the edge of the foundation.**

To use freezer paper, lay the *dull* side of the paper against the *wrong* side of the patch and **press the seam allowance to the shiny side with your iron.**

Patches can be secured to foundations with a *light* dab of glue stick. Don't overdo it.

Match two prepared patches with right sides facing, and whipstitch the edges together with small, close stitches. If the needle nicks the foundations slightly, that's no problem, but don't stitch into them deeply or they will be hard to remove. Also, pull the thread tight so it will not become loose when the foundations are removed.

U P - T O - D A T E   H A N D   P I E C I N G

When the design is complete, remove the basting (if you have used card-stock foundations) and take out the foundations. If your project is large and becomes too heavy as you work, remove the foundations as you go. But don't remove any foundations from patches that have yet to be joined to other patches.

An updated technique for English paper piecing is to iron finished-size freezer paper templates to the wrong side of the fabric before the patches are cut out. Leave at least ½ inch between them, and cut so there is a ¼-inch seam allowance beyond the freezer paper. **You can cut out the patches with either scissors or rotary-cutting equipment.**

Stitch along the edge of the freezer paper with a conventional running stitch. Keep seam allowances free, just as with traditional hand piecing. If the freezer paper lifts during stitching, re-press with an iron or use a pin, fabric glue stick, or quick basting to hold it in place. Adhesive paper, like Con-tact paper, also can be used for this technique, but _remove it before pressing_ as it melts with heat. Press the finished block, following the guidelines in "Pressing for Precision" on page 40.

Inaccurate Blocks

Problem	Solution
Block is too large or too small.	A small error compounded by each patch in a block can affect the size of the block. Check the following to see where the error occurred: **Ruler.** It may have slipped when the seam allowance was measured and cut. **Seam allowances.** They may not be matched correctly. **Stitching.** Inaccurate stitching can cause the seam allowance to run too large or too small. **Templates.** They may have been enlarged by the width of the pencil line used in making them, or the line may have been trimmed away too much.
Block is not square.	This is caused when just a portion of the block is in error or when a pleat was pressed into one of the seams. Check pressing first, then check templates, patches, and seam allowances for the problem.

Skill Builder

Mix techniques for different parts of a block or a quilt.

❏ Combine traditional hand piecing and English paper piecing in the same block to make difficult portions of a block easier to piece.

❏ Mass-produce triangle squares by machine and piece the remainder of the block by hand.

❏ Hand stitch Drunkard's Path curves to control the ease, then machine stitch the blocks together.

❏ Join hand-pieced blocks or add borders by machine.

Try This!

Resealable plastic sandwich bags make it easy to **organize patches for portable piecing kits.** There are two ways to arrange the patches. If you like to complete one block at a time, put the pieces for each block into a separate bag. If you like to complete one step on each block before going on to the next, put the pieces for each step together in a bag. Toss in a spool of matching thread, a packet of needles, and thread snips, label the bag, and you'll be ready to piece at a moment's notice.

Piecing *Glossary*

A

Assembly-line piecing. See *Chain piecing.*

B

Backstitch. A hand or machine stitch made backward over previous stitches in order to strengthen the seam and prevent the thread from unraveling.

Betweens. Short, sturdy needles used for quilting but also preferred by some quilters for hand piecing.

Bias. The stretchy, diagonal grain of the fabric. True bias is at a 45 degree angle to the straight grain, but any off-grain cut may be referred to as a bias cut.

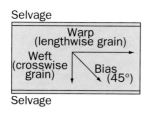

Bias-square triangles. Triangle squares made by sewing bias-cut strips together and then cutting squares from them.

Bleeding. Excess reactive dye that seeps from fibers when fabric is washed. The dye may stain other fabrics.

Block. One unit of a quilt top. A block may be pieced, appliquéd, or a combination of the two.

Butting seams. When aligning two patchwork units for stitching that already have seams in them, it is necessary to butt or nest the existing seam allowances together for a perfect seam intersection.

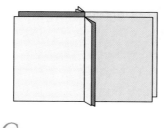

C

Chain piecing. An assembly-line technique where pieces are paired together, then fed through the sewing machine one after another without lifting the presser foot or cutting the threads.

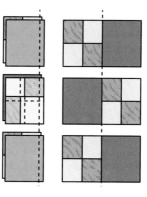

Concave curve. A curve that pushes inward, like a big bite out of a cookie.

Convex curve. A curve that pushes outward, like a wedge cut from a circle or pie.

Concave   Convex

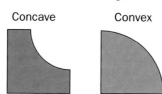

Crazy piecing. Also called crazy quilting. A variety of irregular shapes are sewn to a foundation and often embellished with embroidery, buttons, or other adornments. Crazy piecing often includes fabrics other than cottons, such as velvet, satin, and moiré.

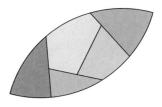

Crocking. When excess dye comes off a piece of dry fabric as it's rubbed against another piece of dry fabric. Also see *Bleeding.*

Crosswise grain. The weft threads, or the straight grain perpendicular to the selvages.

Cutting mat. A protective mat made of self-healing material on which you can safely use a rotary cutter.

D

Design wall. A place to position and shuffle quilt components during the design process. Often made with flannel or batting tacked to a flat wall or foam board.

Dog ears. Little triangles that stick out beyond the raw edge of a block or patchwork

Trim off dog ears

unit when diagonal seams are pressed. They should be trimmed off to reduce bulk in the quilt and to allow for more precise matching.

Drafting. The process of designing a quilt block to fit a desired finished size.

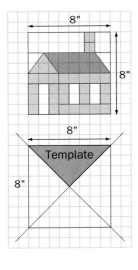

E

Easing. When one patch is longer than another patch it's being sewn to, it is necessary to ease in the extra width or fullness so the patch ends will align. Easing is also necessary for fitting together concave and convex curved pieces.

English paper piecing. A hand-piecing method where individual fabric patches are folded under and basted to finished-size paper templates, then whip-stitched together along their edges. Paper is removed prior to quilting.

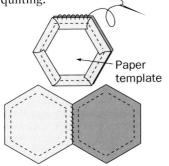

Paper template

Even-feed foot. See *Walking Foot*.

F

Fabric. A quiltmaker's medium. Typically 100 percent cotton, with threads woven tightly enough so that quilting stitches won't fall between the fabric threads.

Fanning. Pressing seam allowances in a circular arrangement to reduce bulk where multiple seams join, such as in an Eight-Pointed Star or Pinwheel block.

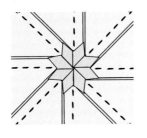

Fat quarter. A quarter yard of fabric that is cut by dividing 1 yard into four large rectangles, each measuring 18 × 22 inches. Fat quarters can be halved in either direction to create fat eighths. Both sizes are often more useful than narrow standard cuts.

Feed dogs. Notched mechanism in the throat plate of a sewing machine that moves up and back the same length as each stitch, gripping the bottom layer of fabric to move it through the machine.

Finger pressing. Using your finger or fingernail to form a temporary crease in the fabric, to press seam allowances aside, or to turn under raw edges.

Finished size. The size of a patch or block after it has been sewn to all neighboring patches. Finished size *does not* include seam allowances.

Foundation piecing. A patchwork technique where the patches in the block are sewn onto a foundation of either fabric or paper. This method enables quilters to work easily with very small pieces, narrow angles, and irregularly shaped pieces, since the foundation helps to stabilize the individual pieces of fabric. Paper foundations are removed before quilting, while fabric foundations remain in the quilt.

Freezer paper. A roll of paper that is plastic-coated on one side. Its original purpose was for freezing foods, but quilters have carried it off to the sewing room for foundation piecing, template making, and appliqué.

G

Grain-line arrow. An arrow printed on a pattern that indicates which direction the template should be placed on the fabric. The grain-line arrow should be parallel to the fabric's straight of grain—either lengthwise or crosswise—for cutting out the piece.

Graph paper. Gridded paper that can be used as foundation material or to draft quilt blocks. It is also helpful in testing for a perfect ¼-inch seam allowance.

Grid-method triangles. Triangle squares made by drawing a grid and diagonal lines on the wrong side of one piece of fabric. The grid is layered on a second piece of fabric with right sides together for sewing. When fabric is stitched and cut apart on the lines, each square of the grid yields two triangle squares.

Hand piecing. Using a running stitch to sew patches of a block together with a hand-held needle and a single strand of thread.

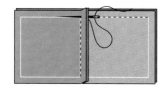

Ironing. Moving an iron back and forth across the surface of yardage to remove wrinkles to prepare it for cutting. See *Pressing.*

Join. As a verb, to sew two pieces, units, or blocks to one another. As a noun, the area where two or more pieces have been joined, such as an eight-seam join in the center of a Pinwheel block.

Lengthwise grain. The warp threads, or the straight of grain parallel to the selvages. This grain direction is the most stable. It is virtually unstretchable.

Loft. Refers to height. The loft of a seam, for example, is the slight ridge formed on the top of patchwork when a seam allowance lies directly underneath. The term is also used when referring to height of batting.

Machine piecing. Sewing pieces of a quilt top together

with a sewing machine. This produces a stronger seam than hand piecing.

Mirror image. The reverse image of a pattern piece. See *Reversed patch.*

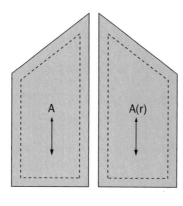

Needles. Use size 11 quilting needles or 80/12 universal machine needles for machine piecing. For hand piecing use sharps or betweens. See *Betweens.*

Patchwork. Small pieces of fabric sewn together into a larger unit, quilt block, or quilt top.

Pivoting. Ending a seam at the intersection of a seam line, so that pieces can be turned and sides realigned to set-in a patch. See *Setting-in.*

Presser foot. The part of the sewing machine that holds fabric layers in place against the throat plate and feed dogs as they approach and pass under the needle.

Pressing. Bringing the weight of an iron straight down on quilt pieces without moving the iron back and forth, in order to flatten seams without stretching or distorting the unit. See *Ironing.*

Quick piecing. Sewing larger pieces of fabric together, such as strip sets or grid triangles, then cutting away smaller, presewn units.

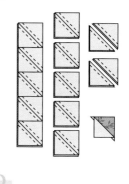

Reversed patch. When asymmetrical pieces are cut as mirror images, they are called reversed patches or pieces. This is often indicated on patterns or templates with an R following the patch name. To cut reverse patches, turn the pattern over or layer two pieces of fabric with right sides facing to cut a regular and reversed patch at the same time.

Rotary cutter. A fabric cutting tool that resembles a pizza cutter, but with a razor-sharp blade capable of slicing through several layers of fabric at once.

Rotary-cutting ruler. Also referred to as a see-through or acrylic ruler, this thick, rigid ruler allows quilters to measure fabric strips and hold them in place securely for rotary cutting.

Running stitch. Short straight stitches, used to hand piece. Longer running stitches are used to baste quilt patches or quilt layers together.

S

Scant seam allowance. Patchwork directions invariably call for a ¼-inch-wide seam allowance. Blocks are more accurate when sewing a seam allowance just slightly less than ¼ inch to account for the amount of fabric lost in the loft of a seam. See *Loft.*

Scissors. Use craft or utility scissors to cut templates, shears to cut fabric, and embroidery scissors or thread snips to trim threads.

Scrap quilt. A quilt made by mixing many different fabrics, rather than by repeating a few fabrics in identical blocks or units.

Seam allowance. The fabric between a stitched seam and the raw edge of patches.

Selvage. Tightly woven, finished edges that run lengthwise along the fabric. They should be trimmed away and not used.

Setting-in. Sewing a patch into an opening between previously stitched pieces of fabric. Also referred to as Y-seam piecing, because the patch arrangement resembles the letter Y.

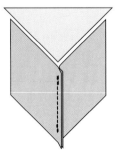

Straight grain. Parallel to either the lengthwise or crosswise threads in a piece of fabric. Also called straight of grain.

String piecing. Creating a customized piece of fabric by sewing together fabric strips of equal or varying widths, sometimes to a foundation material. Patchwork shapes such as squares, triangles, and diamonds can be cut from this fabric.

Strip piecing. Sewing long strips of fabric together lengthwise into a strip set, then cutting away identical, individual segments to be used for patchwork.

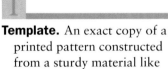

Strip set. Two or more strips of fabric, joined lengthwise. See *Quick piecing.*

T

Template. An exact copy of a printed pattern constructed from a sturdy material like template plastic so that it can be traced around many times onto fabric without distorting its shape.

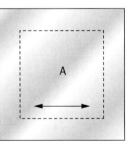

Tension. A sewing machine adjustment that regulates how the bottom and top threads meet in a sewn seam.

Thread. Regular sewing thread used for piecing. Some quilters prefer 100 percent cotton thread, but cotton covered polyester thread is also suitable. Look for "all purpose" or 60 weight thread, as opposed to heavier quilting thread. For piecing, use a neutral-color thread such as gray or tan.

Throat plate. The metal plate of the sewing machine through which the bobbin thread and feed dogs emerge. Available in straight stitch and zigzag stitch models.

Triangle square. A commonly used patchwork unit made up of two right triangles sewn together on their longest edge to form a square. Sometimes referred to as "half-square triangle."

Trimming back. Assembling a larger-than-necessary unit, then trimming it to the correct size before sewing. Often used as a method to enhance accuracy.

U

Unfinished size. The measurement of a patch that includes a ¼-inch seam allowance along each side.

W

Walking foot. Also called an even-feed foot. It works in conjunction with the feed dogs, moving the top fabric in unison with the bottom piece to keep the layers even.

Whipstitch. An overcasting stitch achieved by sliding a hand-held needle through the edges of two patches held right sides together. Used for English paper piecing.

GLOSSARY

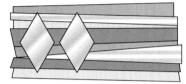

About the Writers

Jane Hall and **Dixie Haywood** are award-winning quiltmakers who are known for adapting traditional designs using contemporary techniques and innovative approaches. Their quilts have been exhibited throughout the country and are in private and public collections. Both have been teaching and judging quiltmaking for over 20 years and have a strong commitment to provide students with well-grounded and creative information so they can make their own unique quilts. They have co-authored *Perfect Pineapples, Precision Pieced Quilts Using the Foundation Method,* and *Firm Foundations.* Dixie is also the author of *The Contemporary Crazy Quilt Project Book* and *Crazy Quilting With A Difference,* and her articles appear regularly in leading quilt periodicals. Jane is a certified appraiser for old and new quilts. Long-time friends, Jane lives in Raleigh, North Carolina, with her husband, Bob, and Dixie lives in Pensacola, Florida, with *her* husband, Bob. They rely heavily on the telephone, FAX, and airlines to function as a team.

Janet Wickell has been quilting for many years, but it became a passion in 1989, when she discovered miniature quilts. She is the sponsor of Minifest, the only national show and seminar devoted to small quilts. For the past several years Janet has been a freelance writer and has contributed to many books for Rodale Press, including eight titles in *The Classic American Quilt Collection* series. She teaches quilting and hand marbling fabric, and she also enjoys herb gardening, photography, and reproducing quilt patterns in stained glass. She is currently working on her first book about miniature quilts. Janet lives in the mountains of western North Carolina with her husband, daughter, and a growing menagerie of animal friends.

Acknowledgments

We gratefully thank the following quiltmakers who graciously permitted us to show their projects as examples of the various piecing techniques described in this book:

Janet Coffman, Crazy-quilted vest on page 108 and Double Wedding Ring quilt on page 90

Stan and Mary Green, antique Grandmother's Flower Garden quilt on page 116

Nancy Johnson-Srebro, Feathered Star on page 28, Eight-Pointed Star on page 80, and Tumbling Blocks quilt on page 76

Tanya Lipinski, Grandmother's Flower Garden blocks on page 116

Samples were made by Karen Soltys, Tanya Lipinski, Suzanne Nelson, Jane Townswick, and Janet Wickell

We also thank the following companies for contributing equipment for the step-by-step photography:

Bernina of America, Inc.—sewing machine

Olfa/O'Lipfa—rotary cutters

Omnigrid, Inc.—rotary cutting mats and rulers

Rowenta—sew 'n press iron

Quilting Styles

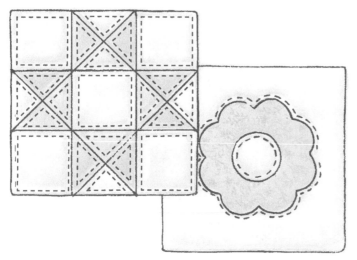

Outline Quilting

Echo Quilting

Single

Double

Crosshatch or Grid Quilting

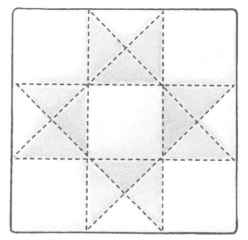

In the Ditch Quilting

Stipple Quilting

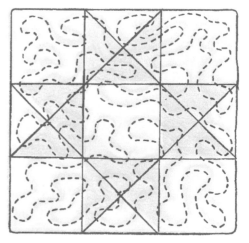

Meander Quilting